The Mennonite Handbook

About "Capped Menno"

Having some fun and depicting Menno Simons with a backward baseball cap indicates that even though our beliefs and practices are serious stuff, we should nonetheless remember that it is not our history and theology that saves us, but Jesus Christ. Therefore, our life in the church can be friendly, and our theological wranglings can be done with a sense of humor and love for our neighbor.

The Mennonite Handbook

Herald Press

Scottdale, Pennsylvania
Waterloo, Ontario

Library of Congress Cataloging-in-Publication Data
The Mennonite handbook.
    p. cm.
    Includes bibliographical references.
    ISBN 978-0-8361-9363-3 (pbk. : alk. paper)
    1. Mennonite Church USA.
    BX8121.3.M46 2007
    289.7—dc22

                        2007001419

Part of this book was originally published as *The Lutheran Handbook* © 2005 Augsburg Fortress.

Scripture quotations are from the New Revised Standard Version Bible, copyright © 1989, Division of Christian Education of the National Council of the Churches of Christ in the United States of America.

Page 61: Illustration by Jan Luyken, *Martyrs Mirror of the Defenseless Christians*, Thieleman J. van Braght (Scottdale, Pa.: Herald Press, 2004), 873. Pages 67–75: Sources for the charts include reference materials from Information Please,® New York Times Public Library/Hyperion, Rose Publishing, Time-Life, and Wadsworth Group/Thomas Learning. Page 81: Map from *Margaret's Print Shop*, Elwood E. Yoder (Scottdale, Pa.: Herald Press, 2005), prepared by Kerry Handel, 14. Page 183: Illustration by Jan Luyken, *Martyrs Mirror of the Defenseless Christians*, Thieleman J. van Braght (Scottdale, Pa.: Herald Press, 2004), 741.

Content editor: Sarah Kehrberg

Cover illustration: Brenda Brown
Interior illustrations: Brenda Brown and Fernando Ruiz
Contributing writers and consultants: David Bergen, Suzanne Burke, Lou Carlozo, Giacomo Cassese, Clarissa P. Gaff, Mark Gardner, Wes Halula, Willmar Harder, Sarah Henrich, Mark Hinton, Sue Houglum, Rolf Jacobson, Hannah Kehr, Esther Koontz, Karl Koop, Susan M. Lang, Andrea Lee, Daniel Levitin, Terry Marks, Catherine Malotky, Anson Miedel, Steven P. Miller, Jeffrey S. Nelson, Rebecca Ninke, Eliseo Pérez-Álvarez, Ron Rempel, John D. Roth, Dawn Rundman, Jonathan Rundman, Brinton Rutherford, Ted Schroeder, Ken Sundet Jones, Hans Wiersma

THE MENNONITE HANDBOOK
Copyright © 2007 by Herald Press, Scottdale, Pa. 15683
    Published simultaneously in Canada by Herald Press,
    Waterloo, Ont. N2L 6H7. All rights reserved
Library of Congress Control Number: 2007001419
International Standard Book Number: 978-0-8361-9363-3
Printed in the United States of America

15 14 13 12 11 10 09 08 07   10 9 8 7 6 5 4 3 2 1

To order or request information, please call 1-800-245-7894, or visit www.heraldpress.com

CONTENTS

Everyday Stuff   83

Bible Stuff

This Book Belongs To

Name _____

Address _____

_____

E-mail _____

Telephone _____

Birth date _____

Baptism or catechism class date _____

Mentors (baptismal sponsors) _____

_____

_____

_____

Churches I've attended   *Years of attendance*

_____   _____

_____   _____

_____   _____

_____   _____

_____   _____

_____   _____

_____   _____

About My Congregation

Name _____

Address _____

_____

Year organized/founded _____

My pastors _____

_____

_____

_____

Number of baptized members _____

Average weekly worship attendance _____

Facts about my denomination _____

_____

_____

Other information about my congregation and faith

_____

_____

_____

PREFACE

Please Be Advised:

Lots of books, pamphlets, and booklets have been written through the centuries as companions for average folks who wanted help navigating their way through a complicated subject. *The Boy Scout Handbook* comes to mind, for example. So do *The American Red Cross First Aid and Safety Handbook, Tune and Repair Your Own Piano,* and *Shakespeare for Dummies.* They stand as testimony to the average person's need for a guide to both the vast truths and complex detail that make up a particular area of interest. These books turn complicated, inaccessible ideas into simple, easy-to-understand concepts and, if necessary, into action steps that are easy to follow.

Likewise, *The Mennonite Handbook* follows this format. Here you will discover a combination of reliable, historical, and theological information alongside some fun facts and very practical tips on being a churchgoing follower of Jesus Christ, all presented in that oh-so-Mennonite, yielded-in-spirit, down-to-earth, tongue-in-cheek sort of way.

You will also discover that this book is intended for learning and enjoyment. It's meant to spur conversation, to inform and edify, and to make you laugh. Think of the book as a comedian with a dry sense of humor and a degree in theology. It can be used in the classroom with students or at the dinner table with family or in solitude.

But however you use it, use it! We've cut the corners off so you can throw it in your backpack or stuff it in a pocket. It's printed on paper that accepts either ink or pencil nicely, so feel free to write and highlight in it (and there's room for notes in the back).

Anyway, the point is this: Being a follower of Jesus is hard enough without having to navigate the faith journey—let alone the maze of church culture—all alone. Sooner or later, everyone needs a companion.

—THE EDITORS

CHURCH STUFF

Every well-prepared Mennonite should have a basic under-standing of church teachings and where they came from.

Plus, since every church goes about worship in a slightly different way, it might take a little time to get the hang of things—especially if you're new to a congregation.

This section includes:

- Essential facts about the Mennonite faith. (If you know these things, you'll know more than most.)

- Practical advice for singing hymns, taking communion, and getting to know the people in your congregation.

- Hints for enjoying worship—even when you're having a bad day.

HOW TO GET TO KNOW YOUR PASTOR

Pastors play an important role in the daily life of your congregation and the community. Despite their churchly calling and Bible knowledge, pastors experience the same kinds of ups and downs as everyone else. They value member efforts to meet, connect with, and support them.

❶ Connect with your pastor after worship.
After the worship service, join others in line to shake the pastor's hand. Sharing a comment about the sermon, readings, or hymns lets the pastor know that his or her worship planning time is appreciated. If your congregation doesn't practice the dismissal line, find other ways to make that personal connection.

❷ Pray daily for your pastor, because he or she doesn't just work on Sunday.
Your pastor has many responsibilities, like visiting members in the hospital, writing sermons, and figuring out who can help drain the flooded church basement. In your prayers, ask God to grant your pastor health, strength, and wisdom to face the many challenges of leading a congregation.

❸ Ask your pastor to share with you why he or she entered ordained ministry.
There are many reasons why a pastor may have started on the journey to become a minister. Be prepared for a story that may surprise you.

4 Stop by your pastor's office to talk, or consider making an appointment to get to know him or her.

Pastors welcome the opportunity to connect with church members at times other than worship. As you would with any drop-in visit, be sensitive to the fact that your pastor may be quite busy. A scheduled appointment just to chat could provide a welcome break in your pastor's day.

5 Offer to help.

Working side by side with your pastors may be the best way to get to know them. This could be through serving on the worship planning committee together, or raking leaves in their front lawn. Be creative!

Getting to know your pastors can help you to get more out of church.

HOW TO SURVIVE FOR ONE HOUR IN AN UN-AIR-CONDITIONED CHURCH

Getting trapped in an overheated building is never a positive churchgoing experience. The key is to minimize your heat gain and electrolyte loss.

❶ Plan ahead.
When possible, scout out the building ahead of time to locate optimal seating near fans or open windows. Consider where the sun will be during the worship service and avoid sitting under direct sunlight. Bring a bottle of water for each person in your group.

❷ Maintain your distance from others.
Human beings disperse heat and moisture as a means of cooling themselves. An average-size person puts off about as much heat as a 75-watt lightbulb. The front row will likely be empty and available.

❸ Remain still.
Fidgeting will only make your heat index rise.

Use your bulletin as a personal fan to keep cool.

4 **Think cool thoughts.**
Your mental state can affect your physical disposition. If the heat distracts you from worship, imagine you're sitting on a big block of ice.

5 **Dress for survival.**
Wear only cool, breathable fabrics.

6 **Be involved in the service.**
Serving as worship leader or usher will excuse you from sitting in a crowded pew, and the responsibilities will help keep your mind off the heat.

On hot days put your name in to be usher.

7 **Pray.**
Jesus survived on prayer in the desert for 40 days. Lifting and extending your arms in an open prayer position may help cool your body by dispersing excess heat. If you've been perspiring, though, avoid exposing others to your personal odor.

Be Aware

• Carry a personal fan—or use your bulletin as a substitute.

• Worship services scheduled for one hour sometimes will run long. Plan ahead.

HOW TO RESPOND WHEN SOMEONE SITS IN YOUR SEAT

Human beings are creatures of habit. There is something so comforting about putting the left shoe on before the right; reading a story, singing Teddy a song, and *then* getting in bed; coming to church and sitting in the fifth row back on the left side. Human beings are also territorial in nature and sometimes see strangers in their space as an affront. These situations need not be cause for alarm.

❶ Smile and greet the "intruders."
Oftentimes they are visitors to your congregation—new blood. Avoid creating bad blood you might regret later on. Make solid eye contact so they know you mean it, shake hands with them, and leave no impression that they've done something wrong.

❷ View the "intrusion" as an opportunity.
Remember, you don't own the pew or that row of chairs; you just borrow it once a week. Take the opportunity to get out of your rut and sit someplace new. This will physically emphasize a change in your perspective and may yield new spiritual discoveries.

❸ If you can tell that your new friends feel uncomfortable at having displaced you, despite your efforts to the contrary, make an extra effort to welcome them.
Consider inviting them to lunch after church to become acquainted. If you were planning on having leftovers or cold cereal, consider inviting them to an inexpensive local restaurant.

HOW TO SURVIVE AN ESPECIALLY LONG AND PERSONAL SHARING TIME

The church body is a community of believers that, among other things, share each other's burdens and cares (Galatians 6:2; James 5:16). This is often done formally on Sunday morning during Sharing Time, when anyone can stand and respond to the sermon, give an announcement, or share something from their personal life and past week.

Sharing Time can be a deeply moving time as individuals bring their joys and concerns to their brothers and sisters in Christ. It can also be uncomfortable for those who are not used to the baring of souls in public, tedious if someone is long-winded, and can be downright inappropriate, depending on the subject matter. The goal is to maintain an attitude of genuine caring.

❶ **Give the inappropriate sharer the benefit of the doubt.**
Sometimes people get carried away or lose their judgment for various reasons. It can happen to anyone, including you, so try and keep an open mind.

❷ **Remain polite and respectful.**
If this becomes impossible, subtly catch up on your bulletin announcement reading. It may be a good idea to keep a hymn book open to a favorite hymn so you can prayerfully ponder the words. Do not roll your eyes, yawn, or take out any electronic devices.

❸ **Sometimes an individual becomes notorious in the inappropriate use of Sharing Time.**
When that happens, it may become necessary to speak the truth in love (Ephesians 4:15).

The Long-Winded Sharer

- *Your Problem*: This is generally hard to notice in yourself. However, to be prepared, practice any sharing you plan to do ahead of time. Time yourself and keep your statement to 2-3 minutes. Use notes during your sharing to avoid rambling. If the Spirit moves you during the service, make a conscious effort to keep it brief.

- *Someone Else's Problem*: First contact your pastor and state your concern. The pastor or someone else in the congregation may have already approached the offender, and there is no reason to be the second in line. If your pastor commissions you, find a kind way to express your opinion (see "How to Resolve Interpersonal Conflict," pages 114-15). Note: Never confront someone in front of others. You don't want to unduly embarrass anyone.

The Inappropriate Sharer

- *Your Problem*: It is best to avoid the following: anything of a sexual nature, politics, personal soapboxes, and family/vocation/recreational bragging. If at all in doubt, consult your pastor or another sister or brother in the church.

- *Someone Else's Problem*: Follow the steps given above.

The Too-Frequent Sharer

- *Your Problem*: A good rule of thumb is to keep your uninvited sharing time to once a month. Sometimes the pastor or worship leader may request your participation in the service that requires personal sharing—this doesn't technically count, but should be taken into consideration.

- *Someone Else's Problem*: Direct confrontation with this kind of sharer will probably only result in your becoming part of their next sharing. There is clearly a need here that is not being met. Consider inviting this person to coffee or lunch once a week or to join your small group.

HOW TO USE A
WORSHIP BULLETIN

Many Mennonite congregations offer a printed resource called
a bulletin to assist worshipers. The bulletin may contain the
order of the service, music listings, the day's Bible readings,
and important community announcements.

❶ Arrive early.
   A few extra minutes before worship will allow you to scan
   the bulletin and prepare for the service.

❷ Receive the bulletin from the usher.
   When you enter the worship space, an usher will give you a
   bulletin. Some congregations stack bulletins near the
   entrance for self-service.

❸ Review the order of worship.
   When seated, open the bulletin and find the order of the
   service, usually printed on the first or second page.

❹ Determine if other worship resources are required.
   The order of worship may specify additional hymnals, song
   sheets, candles, or other external supplies required during
   the service.

❺ Fill out the attendance card or register.
   A card may be located inside the bulletin or somewhere in
   your row. Fill it out completely. You may be asked to pass
   this card to an usher or to place it in the offering plate.
   Some congregations have visitors/communion attendance
   books for people to sign.

6 Reflect on bulletin artwork.

Covers often feature a drawing or design that corresponds to the season of the church year or the day's Bible verses. Examine the artwork and make a note of its connection to the lessons or sermon.

7 Track your worship progress.

The bulletin will guide you through the hymns, Scripture readings, and prayers as you worship and let you know where you are at all times.

8 Watch for worship dialogues.

The bulletin may contain parts of the service not found in the hymnal or other worship resource. The worship leader's parts may be marked with a "P:" or "L:". The congregation's responses may be marked with a "C:" and are often printed in boldface type.

9 Identify the worship leaders and assistants.

The names of ushers, song leaders, greeters, readers, worship leader, and pastors usually can be found in the bulletin. Greet these people by name following the service. Make good eye contact.

10 Review the printed announcements.

Community activities, calendars, and updates are often listed in the back of the bulletin. Scan listings during the prelude music, the offering, or the spoken announcements.

11 Make good use of the bulletin after the service.

Some congregations re-use bulletins; if so, you may want to return the bulletin. Recycling bins may also be provided. If you wish, you may take the bulletin home with you for mid-week activities.

Be Aware

• Bulletins often use abbreviations to signify which hymnals should be used if more than one is used on a regular basis. Look at the different hymnals before worship starts, if possible, and make an educated guess. If you find yourself on the wrong song, guess again. (For example, *Hymnal: A Worship Book* is often abbreviated *HWB*.)

• Many church secretaries and worship committees need help preparing the bulletin each week. You may want to volunteer to copy, fold, or assemble the bulletin for an upcoming service.

• Most congregations stand at certain times during worship, such as during the opening hymns or for a special prayer. Standing and sitting aren't for exercise. Rather, they're an important physical participation in worship that helps you focus on the meaning or sing vigorously.

If you choose not to use your worship bulletin, be sure to recycle it whenever possible.

HOW TO SING A FOUR-PART HYMN

Music is an important part of the Mennonite tradition and an enjoyable way to build community. Hymn singing can be done without demonstrable emotion, but many otherwise stoic Mennonites appropriately channel emotion into their hymn singing and are therefore loud.

1 Locate hymns in advance.
As you prepare for worship, consult the worship bulletin or the hymn board to find numbers for the day's hymns. Bookmark these pages in the hymnal using an offering envelope or attendance card.

2 Familiarize yourself with the hymns.
Examine the composer credits, the years the composer(s) lived, and whether the tune has a different name than the hymn itself. Note how the hymn is categorized in the hymnal. Many hymnals group the songs into categories, such as "Praise and Worship" and "Christmas."

3 Assist nearby visitors or children.
Using a hymnal can be confusing. If your neighbor seems disoriented, help them find the correct pages, or let them read from your book.

4 Share your hymnal when needed.
If a row or pew is filled, you will most likely need to share your hymnal with someone else. If they offer, allow them to hold half of the book. If they don't, hold the book over toward them so they can easily see the page being sung.

5 Adopt a posture for best vocal performance.
Hold the hymnal away from your body at chest level. Place
one hand under the spine of the binding, leaving the other
hand free to turn the pages. Keep your chin up so your
voice projects outward.

6 Begin singing.
If the hymn is unfamiliar, sing the melody for the first
verse. If you read music, explore the harmony parts during
the remaining verses. If you do not read music, listen for
the good singers and try to sit near them in the future
(without it seeming too obvious). Loud-singing neighbors
may or may not be in tune, so follow them with caution.

7 Focus on the hymn's content.
Some of the lyrics may connect with a Scripture reading of
the day. Certain ones may be especially inspiring. Many
hymns are poems set to music. Don't be afraid to enjoy the
beauty of the words.

8 Avoid dreariness.
Hymns are often sung in such a serious way that the
congregation forgets to enjoy the music. Sing with energy
and feeling.

9 Follow the song leader.
You come to church to sing with others. Regardless of
whether you like the song leader's style or believe their
skills to be adequate, humble yourself (*Gelassenheit*) and
submit to their leadership if just for this church service.

Be Aware

- Hymnals are not just for use at church. Consider keeping a personal copy of your congregation's hymnal at home for further reference and study. Hymnals also make excellent baptism, birthday, Christmas, or graduation gifts.

- Some hymns use words and phrases that are difficult to understand (such as, "Here I raise my Ebenezer," from the hymn "Come Thou Fount of Every Blessing"). Use a dictionary or a Bible with a concordance to clear up any uncertainty.

Support the hymnal's spine with one hand. Place the other on the open page.

HOW TO SING A PRAISE SONG

Many Mennonite congregations use worship styles, featuring guitars and drums. In these settings the words are typically displayed on large multimedia projection screens.

❶ Follow the instructions of the song leader.
Someone in the praise band will invite the congregation to stand up, sit down, repeat certain sections, or divide into men's and women's vocal parts. Pay attention to this person to avoid getting off track.

❷ Learn the melody and song structure.
Pay special attention to the melody line sung by the band's lead vocalist. Praise songs can be tricky because they are rarely printed with notated sheet music and are sung differently from place to place.

❸ Sing along with gusto.
Once the melody has been introduced, join in the singing. When you're comfortable with the song, experiment with harmony parts.

❹ Avoid "zoning out."
Singing lyrics that are projected on giant screens can result in a glazed-over facial expression. Avoid this by surveying the worship area and making eye contact with other people.

❺ Identify lyrical themes.
Determine if the song is being used as a confession, a prayer, a hymn of praise, or serves another purpose.

6 Watch out for raised hands.

Some Mennonites emote while singing contemporary Christian songs and may suddenly raise their hands in praise to God. Be sure to give these worshipers plenty of room.

Be Aware

• Mennonite worship is highly participatory. The praise band is there to help you and the congregation to sing and participate in worship, not to perform a concert.

• Although there are no prohibitions in the Mennonite tradition against physical expression during worship, in some congregations praise gestures will draw amused stares.

Beware of especially passionate worshipers who might raise their hands too quickly.

HOW TO LISTEN TO A SERMON

Mennonites believe an important way God's Word comes to us is through preaching from the Bible, as well as communal study and interpretation of the Scriptures. Honoring God's Word, not to mention getting something out of church, includes diligent listening to the sermon and active mental participation.

Note: "God's Word," "Bible," and "Scripture" are all synonymous.

❶ Review active listening skills.
While the listener in this case doesn't get to speak, the sermon is still a conversation. Make mental notes as you listen. Take notice of where and why you react and which emotions you experience.

❷ Take notes.
Note-taking promotes active listening and provides a good basis for later reflection. It also allows you to return to confusing or complicated parts at your own leisure. Some congregations provide space in the bulletin for notes. In a pinch, the margins can work as well.

Take notes to recall more information and get more out of the sermon.

Try taking notes in an outline form so you can keep up without missing good information.

❸ Maintain good posture. Avoid slouching.
Sit upright with your feet planted firmly on the ground and your palms on your thighs. Beware of the impulse to slouch, cross your arms, or lean against your neighbor, since these can encourage drowsiness.

❹ Expect to be convicted.
You may feel an emotional pinch when the preacher names the sinner in you. Pay attention to your reaction, and open yourself emotionally rather than becoming defensive. This is how you grow as a Christian.

❺ Accept God's grace.
In some form or another the preacher will remind you of the hope we have through Jesus Christ. You may feel a physical lightness, as though you've set down a great burden. You may cry tears of joy. This is normal.

6 Determine to change.

The preacher will most likely give encouragement and suggestions for change and/or renewal in your life. Each day begins anew; determine to be a better person, starting now.

7 Respond.

Many churches include a sharing time in their worship service. If the Holy Spirit is moving in especially powerful ways, consider sharing your thoughts or insights on the sermon with the congregation. (See "How to Survive a Particularly Long and Personal Sharing Time," pages 21-22 for guidelines.)

8 Review alone and with community.

If you've taken written notes, read through them later that day or the next day and consider corresponding with the preacher if you have questions or need clarification. If you've taken mental notes, review them in a quiet moment. Create review time with others in your congregation or household on a weekly basis.

HOW TO RESPOND TO A DISRUPTION DURING WORSHIP

Disruptions during worship are inevitable. The goal is to soften their impact.

❶ Simply ignore the offending event, if possible.
Many disruptions are brief, and the persons involved act quickly to quiet them. Avoid embarrassing others; maintain your attention on the worship activity.

❷ Some disruptions cannot be ignored and may threaten to continue indefinitely. The agony will go on unless you act. Consider the following types:

Active Children

- *Your Problem*: You are most familiar with your own family. If you sense an outburst will end quickly, simply allow it to pass. If not, escort the child to the lobby for a little quiet time, then return.

Note: Under all circumstances, children should be made to feel welcome in worship!

Try to ignore worship interruptions you think will end soon.

- *Someone Else's Problem*: Politely offer to help, perhaps by helping to entertain the child quietly or—with the parents' permission—by escorting the tot to the lobby or nursery.

Personal Electronics

Turn off all personal electronic devices before worship.

- *Your Problem*: Turn off cell phones, pagers, and other electronic alarms immediately and discreetly. If contact is made and it is critical, remove yourself to the lobby and call back. Under no circumstances should you answer your phone during worship.

- *Someone Else's Problem*: Politely ask them to respect worship by moving the conversation to the lobby.

Chatty Neighbor

- *Your Problem*: Be alert to stares and grim looks from neighbors, and be prepared to stop talking upon seeing them.

- *Someone Else's Problem*: Politely ask the talkers to wait until after worship to conclude the conversation. During the coffee hour, approach them with a cookie or cup of coffee to mend any offense they may have felt.

Cameras

- *Your Problem*: Ask first if cameras are allowed. If so, unobtrusively and discreetly position yourself out of the line of sight of other worshipers. Be aware of the film's exposure number to avoid jarring auto-rewind noises.

- *Someone Else's Problem*: Politely offer to show the photographer where to stand to get the shot but without obstructing worship.

Sound System Feedback

- Pastors often make jokes to cover for feedback and keep the appropriate mood for worship. If this happens, consider making a donation earmarked for a "new sound system" in the plate.

THE ANATOMY OF A BAPTISM

Pouring water on the baptized person, the pastor says, "I baptize you in the name of the Father, and of the Son, and of the Holy Spirit."

An elder in the church, parent, or spiritual mentor assists in the baptizing ceremony.

Parents and friends are on hand to support those being baptized. The whole congregation often joins in pledging support and guidance.

The heads of those being baptized are bowed. They kneel to show submission to God and the church.

A towel is provided to dry the head and neck of those being baptized.

After being sprinkled with water, the pastor helps the baptizees to their feet saying, ". . . in the name of Christ and the church, I give you my hand and bid you to rise and walk in newness of life. . . ."

Mennonites believe in threefold baptism: Spirit, water, and blood. Baptism by Spirit refers to the gift of the Holy Spirit; water (pictured here) is the earthly element of baptism, a symbol of God's washing the sin away; baptism by blood makes reference to an individual's commitment to their new life, even unto death. These three baptisms do not happen all at once. Generally the water baptism is the final step, a public confirmation that the first two have taken place.

Baptism is received as a sign that a person has repented, received forgiveness, renounced evil, and died to sin, through the grace of God in Christ Jesus.

By choosing to become baptized, the baptized are not only making a public confession of faith and loyalty to walking in the way of Jesus, but also promising that they will be an active and engaged member in their congregation and the greater Mennonite church.

On January 21, 1525 a group of radical adults met together in Zurich, Switzerland, and performed the first rebaptism of adults in the Anabaptist movement. This was done behind closed doors and in secret. Today, in the United States and Canada, most baptisms are performed openly and publicly.

HOW TO RECEIVE COMMUNION

Communion, sometimes called the Lord's Supper or the Eucharist (Luke 22:7-23), is an important and often emotional event in Mennonite worship. Communion is not celebrated weekly in Mennonite congregations. Some congregations have communion once a month and others only twice a year. The basics of communion are always the same: eating the bread and drinking the grape juice. But how this is done changes from church to church and from time to time. It's wise to be both mentally and spiritually alert.

Verbal directions will most likely be given. Some congregations commune by passing the bread and individual cups throughout the pews or chairs, some practice "continuous communion" with bread and wine stations, some stand in a circle and the church members serve each other, and some come up with even more creative ways. Below are two of the most common.

Continuous Communion

❶ Look for guidance from the usher.
The usher will direct the people in each row or pew to stand and get in line.

❷ Proceed to the communion station.
The best practice is often simply to follow the person in front of you and do what they do.

When receiving the bread, cup your hands so the bread will not roll out.

❸ Receive the bread.
Extend your hands with palms facing up. After the server places the bread in your open hands,

grasp the piece with the fingers of one hand. When the server says, "The body of Christ, given for you," eat the bread.

Note: Sometimes the bread is still in loaf form and you are expected to tear a piece off yourself.

4 Receive the grape juice.
Take a filled cup from the tray. When the server says, "The blood of Christ, shed for you," drink the juice.

Note: Most Mennonites do not use wine in their communion service. This is because Mennonites do not traditionally drink alcoholic beverages.

5 Return the empty cup.
It may be necessary for you to carry the empty cup over to a plate or basket on the way back to your seat.

6 Return to your seat.
This is an appropriate time to close your eyes, pray, or listen to the communion music. Resist the temptation to stare at other worshipers proceeding to communion. This is not a fashion show.

Seated Communion
1 Receive the bread.
The servers will pass the bread throughout the congregation. It will most likely already be cut up, but if the bread is still in loaf form, simply tear off a small piece and pass it on. The baskets of bread should be passed in a similar style to a communion plate.

❷ Receive the grape juice.
The servers will pass around the trays with individual cups in them. Select one and pass the tray to next person. Try not to look for the cup with the most grape juice in it.

❸ Wait for the pastor to give the signal to eat and drink.
In this style of communion everyone eats and drinks together. The pastor will say something like, "Let us partake together." If you accidentally eat the bread or drink the juice prematurely, REMAIN CALM. Share with your neighbor or pretend to chew/swallow.

Be Aware

• Unless stated otherwise, children and unbaptized persons should not participate in communion, although they are encouraged to observe and worship with the congregation during the service. Christians of other denominations are welcome to partake.

• Pastoral blessings and/or grapes are often available for children.

• After receiving the bread and wine, avoid saying, "Thank you" to the server. The body and blood are gifts from God. If you wish, a gentle "Amen" is appropriate.

HOW TO WASH FEET

This ritual was given by Jesus during the Last Supper (John 13:1-17). This act of servanthood is a special time for church members to humble themselves before each other as they remember how Jesus humbled himself by going to the cross. This is usually only done once or twice a year, often in connection with communion, and can be a very emotional and spiritual experience. It is important to keep this in mind, because it can also be a deeply uncomfortable process.

❶ **Pay close attention to any special spoken or written instructions.**
When everyone is at their most vulnerable, it is not helpful to do something out of order or not as specified.

Hold your partner's foot firmly while gently splashing it once or twice with water.

❷ Pick an appropriate partner.
Washing your best friend's feet has a high risk of ending in giggling. It is probably best to pick someone you don't know well but respect. Traditionally churches separated the males from the females for foot washing, but this is not always the case. If you are more comfortable washing the feet of someone from your own gender, by all means do so.

❸ Wear appropriate clothing.
Females should avoid all hosiery (sheer or cotton) unless it is knee length and easily removed. Try to select shoes and sock combinations that produce the least sweating and offensive odor.

❹ Practice good hygiene on the day of foot washing.
It is best to wash your feet within two hours of the foot washing ceremony. Foot washing is merely symbolic. Be sure your toenails are trimmed.

❺ Keep the ritual short and sweet.
Foot washing consists of gently splashing each of your partner's feet with water and then patting them dry with a towel. It should not take longer than a few minutes. After both pairs of feet have been washed, the partners hug each other (if you have traditionalist leanings, go ahead and kiss each other) and say something like "God's peace sister/brother."

❻ Maintain an attitude of quiet respect.
No talking is needed, so you can take this time to pray and mediate on servanthood if the room is quiet. On the other hand, some foot washing rooms are filled with low-level friendly chattering and visiting in which case, join in.

Be Aware

- Wait to put your shoes back on until both partner's feet are washed and the dismissing hug has taken place. To do it in the middle breaks the flow of the ritual and can make for a long awkward moment.

- If you are feeling very nervous about the whole ordeal, practice. Ask to wash the feet of someone you trust. There is nothing like doing it once to get those initial butterflies in control.

- Holding the bare foot of a venerated elder in the church can be quite uncomfortable and humbling, but this is, after all, the point of foot washing. The greater the risks you take and the more you invest emotionally, the greater the spiritual rewards.

HOW TO PASS THE PLATE

The offering is a practice that dates back to Old Testament times, linking money and personal finance directly to one's identity as a child of God. Giving of one's financial resources is an integral part of a healthy faith life.

❶ Pay close attention to instructions, if any.
The worship leader may announce the method of offering, or instructions may be printed in the worship bulletin or projected on an overhead screen.

❷ Be alert for the plate's arrival at your row or pew.
Keep an eye on the ushers, if there are any. In most congregations, guiding and safeguarding the offering plate is their job, so wherever they are, so is the plate. As the plate approaches you, set aside other activity and prepare for it.

❸ Avoid watching your neighbor or making judgments about their offering.
Many people contribute once a month by mail and some by automatic withdrawal from a bank account. If your neighbor passes the plate to you without placing an envelope, check, or cash in it, do not assume they didn't contribute.

❹ Place your offering in the plate as you pass it politely to the next person.
Do not attempt to make change from the plate if your offering is in cash. Avoid letting the plate rest in your lap as you finish writing a check. Simply pass it on and hand your check to an usher as you leave at the end of worship. Many churches provide envelopes for privacy purposes.

❺ Be sensitive to idiosyncrasies in plate types.
Some congregations use traditional, wide-rimmed, felt-lined, brass-plated offering plates. Some use baskets of varying types, and some use cloth bags. And some don't pass anything; the congregation is invited to walk up front and bring their offerings—often while singing.

Be Aware

- Your church offering may be tax deductible, as provided by law. Consider making your offering by check or automatic withdrawal; you will receive a statement from your church in the first quarter of the next year.

- Mennonite churches generally depend entirely upon the money that comes in through congregational offerings. Many members work toward tithing as a putting-your-money-where-your-mouth-is expression of faith. (The term tithing means "one-tenth" and refers to the practice of giving 10 percent of one's gross income to support the church's work.)

- Offerings are not fees or dues given out of obligation. They are gifts of thanksgiving returned to God from the heart.

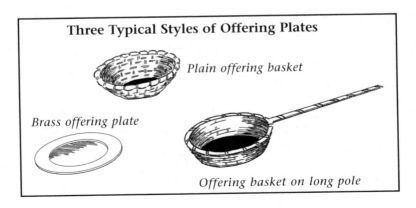

Three Typical Styles of Offering Plates

Plain offering basket

Brass offering plate

Offering basket on long pole

HOW TO GREET YOUR NEIGHBOR

Mennonites speak of the church as a gathered community. Many church services thus involve a formal time to greet neighbors, as well as to worship God. The two—loving God and loving your neighbor—go hand-in-hand.

For some, greeting time can be awkward due to its free-for-all nature. Some also feel uncomfortable because of their fear of being hugged. You can survive greeting time, however, with these steps.

❶ Pay attention.
Greeting time is not always listed in the printed bulletin. The worship leader will, however, give a verbal cue and perhaps even a prescriptive phrase to use (see #6).

❷ Adopt a peaceful frame of mind.
Clear your mind of distracting and disrupting thoughts so you can participate joyfully.

❸ Determine the appropriate form of safe touch.
Handshaking is most common. Be prepared, however, for hugs, half-hugs, one-armed hugs, pats, and other forms of physical contact. Nods are appropriate for distances greater than two pews or rows.

❹ Be welcoming to everyone.
Welcoming time can sometimes be lonely for guests. Don't just greet your good friends. Make an effort to seek out new faces. This is not the time for extended introductions, but perhaps invite them to Sunday school, coffee time, or lunch.

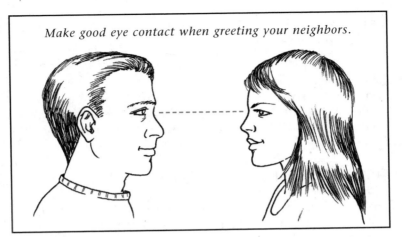

Make good eye contact when greeting your neighbors.

5 Make appropriate eye contact.

Look the other person in the eye but do not stare. The action of looking the person in the eye engages them and lets them know you really care.

6 Greet your neighbor.

Mennonites do not use a formal greeting. The worship leader may supply you with a phrase, or you can use such common acceptable expressions as, "Welcome," "So glad to see you here," "God be with you," or "The peace of God." Don't linger in extraneous chitchat. Move on to the next person.

Be Aware

• Because Mennonites are a small denomination with many family relationships, they may ask questions about your relatives or acquaintances. They are generally simply trying to be friendly—even if the questions may be inappropriate or irritating.

HOW TO STAY ALERT IN CHURCH

❶ Get adequate sleep.
Late Saturday nights are Sunday morning's worst enemy. Resolve to turn in earlier. A good night's sleep on Friday night is equally important to waking rested on Sunday, since sleep debt builds up over time.

❷ Drink plenty of water, though not too much.
It is easier to remain alert when you are well hydrated. Consider keeping a small bottle of water with you during worship. One quick bathroom break is considered permissible. Two or more are bad form.

❸ Eat a high-protein breakfast.
Foods high in carbohydrates force your body to metabolize them into sugars, which can make you drowsy. If your diet allows, eat foods high in protein instead, such as scrambled eggs with bacon.

❹ Arrive early and find the coffee pot.
If you don't drink coffee, consider a caffeinated soda.

❺ Focus on your posture.
Sit up straight with your feet planted firmly on the floor. Avoid slouching, as this encourages sleepiness. Good posture will promote an alert bearing and assist in paying attention, so you'll get more out of worship.

❻ If you have difficulty focusing on the service, divert your attention. Occupy your mind, not your hands.
Look around the worship space for visual stimuli. Keep your mind active in this way while continuing to listen.

❼ Stay alert by flexing muscle groups in a pattern.
Clench toes and feet; flex calf muscles, thighs, glutei, abdomen, hands, arms, chest, and shoulders. Repeat. Avoid shaking, rocking, or other movements that attract undue attention.

❽ If all else fails, consider pinching yourself.
Dig your nails into the fleshy part of your arm or leg, pinch yourself, bite down on your tongue with moderate pressure. Try not to cry out.

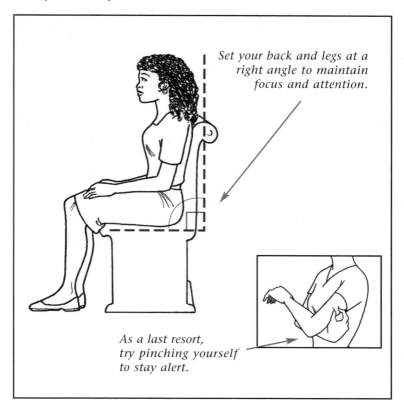

Set your back and legs at a right angle to maintain focus and attention.

As a last resort, try pinching yourself to stay alert.

WHAT TO BRING TO A CHURCH POTLUCK

Any Mennonite church worth attending has a potluck or fellowship meal at least a few times a year. Below are some hints for getting you through your first (or sixty-seventh) church potluck.

1 Bring one dish, but make plenty.
Enjoy the break from preparing a well-rounded, complete nutritional meal for your family. If your family or group is particularly large, you may want to make two dishes. Resist the urge to use this as an excuse to clean out your refrigerator. Make something you are good at, and make a lot so all can have a helping.

2 Don't try a dish for the first time on potluck day.
Stick with something you know how to prepare well. This will ensure an empty serving dish on the way home, which is easier to clean and lifts the spirits of any cook.

3 Pick a dish that is potluck friendly.
• Can it be easily transported out of the house, in and out of the car, and into your eating space?

• Can you make a lot of it without too much fuss?

• Does it work on a plastic plate? (i.e. don't bring soup unless you are providing the soup bowls).

• What are your dish's heating and cooling needs? Can your church kitchen meet those needs?

• Will your dish excessively hold up the line? (e.g. fajitas, tacos, or other dishes that take some kind of assembly).

4 Be creative.

With a little forethought and brainstorming you will be amazed at the variety of dishes you can prepare. Don't stick with the same old casseroles and salads. This is the time to strut your cuisine-stuff.

5 Try a little of everything.

It is generally considered bad potluck manners to take a whole bunch of one dish (particularly one of the popular dishes). Sample half portions of many dishes. This results in everyone getting to try their favorite food, everyone's dish at least being tried (oh, the stigma of the uncracked casserole top), and the "potluck puddle"—that wonderful mix of food that happens only on a potluck plate.

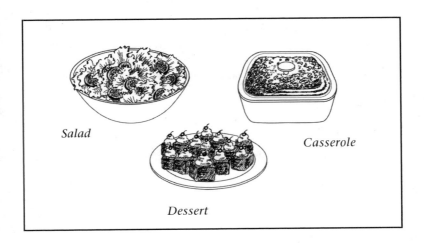

Salad

Casserole

Dessert

Be Aware

- To use a recipe from the Mennonite Central Committee World Community Cookbook Series (*Simply in Season, More-with-Less* or *Extending the Table*) would be experimental in some circles, but is a safe choice among Mennonites.

- Another obvious resource is Phyllis Pellman Good's book called *The Best of Mennonite Fellowship Meals.*

- Any combination of flavored gelatin, shredded carrots, mini-marshmallows, cottage cheese, and canned pears is an acceptable "utility" dish.

- It is considerate to consider people's various food allergies and preferences. Consider not using nut products, wheat, milk, eggs, and/or meat in your potluck dish.

HOW TO SURVIVE A CHURCH SPLIT

The Anabaptist movement was never a single church. As a grassroots religious movement it had various important leaders, sprang up in different areas of Europe, and had differing beliefs. Anabaptists and their Mennonite descendants are deeply religious and passionate people. They often hold strong convictions, sometimes even stridently so. They are suspicious of centralized control. Given this religious alchemy, the last 500 years has produced a good number of church splits.

Unity is better so of course church splits are to be avoided as a general rule. Splits can be devastating and complex, and your very salvation may be called into question. But sometimes church splits can't be avoided. You may inherit a church split, or you may find yourself in the middle of one in progress. The tips found below merely represent a starting point to help you find growth in a painful situation.

When You Inherit a Church Split

❶ Don't make a big issue of it.

People may wonder why some Mennonites wear bonnets and black hats but your church looks modern and high tech. Tell these people, and yourself, that the world may actually be more colorful because there are a variety of customs and convictions. If they are still not convinced, tell them that the Lord looks on the heart.

❷ Respect the various churches and conferences and allow them to have integrity.

They often have decades or centuries of history. Once you have chosen or inherited a place, stand firm. Resist the temptation to jump ship for personal gain or a nicer church building.

❸ Call the other groups by their own chosen names.
Do this even if they are somewhat unusual, such as the
New Testament Mennonite Church. Especially avoid giving
them undesirable names such as black bumpers, worldly,
fundies, peewees, or liberal apostates.

❹ Allow the possibility that the split may heal.
A number of Anabaptist and Mennonite groups have
merged at the same time that new groups are forming. Try
to think positively that with time a division may heal.

When You Find Yourself in a Church Split
❶ Choose your side carefully.
Should baptism be by a sprinkling of water, partial
immersion, or full immersion? Should an erring member
be shunned? Are business contracts really a mortal sin? Are
movie theaters the house of Satan? These are issues not to
be taken lightly. Much prayer and discussion are needed.

**❷ Don't break social contact with your former brothers
and sisters in Christ.**
Jesus hung around with sinners a lot. Just because you
disagree doesn't mean you can't live together (usually). You
may want to avoid the topics that split your church, but
otherwise you probably have just as much in common with
them as before.

❸ Be generous.

If you are part of the group that is staying (feeling attacked and a bit self-righteous), don't hoard the hymnals or church silverware. Many of the departing group probably spent as many hours using those items as you have. If you are part of the group that is breaking away (feeling attacked and a bit self-righteous), resist the temptation to plunder as you flee. It comes close to stealing by most definitions.

❹ Continue to pray and think positively of your departed brothers and sisters.

God still loves them and so should you. If you find it hard to mention their names out loud, start with euphemisms (try to keep them positive) and then move to initials. You may be surprised how God will work in your heart.

FIVE IMPORTANT THINGS THE MENNONITE LEADERS WROTE AND WHY THEY'RE STILL IMPORTANT TODAY

❶ **"The Schleitheim Confession"**
In 1527 a crucial meeting of Anabaptist leaders convened in Schleitheim, Switzerland. In the midst of fundamental agreements a consensus of seven points emerged. This confession of faith, written in language for all to understand, became a powerful testimony that peace is a way of life and gave substance to a movement that had been largely fragmented and without a central focus and structure. Michael Sattler, a former Benedictine monk turned Anabaptist leader, is often credited as being the author. To read a more complete summary of the Confession, see pages 180-81.

❷ *The Martyrs Mirror*
Dutch Mennonite pastor Thieleman J. van Braght compiled the story of fifteen centuries of Christian martyrdom from the time of Christ to 1660 AD in response to the comfortable and prosperous life Dutch Mennonites were experiencing in the late 1600s. He felt this new peace and prosperity was causing them to lose their Anabaptist faith. Van Braght collected the accounts of martyrdom with the hope that they would inspire the reader to hold as steadfastly to the faith as did the martyrs of whom he wrote. Such a faith, worthy of so dear a price, is worthy of perpetuation and should serve to challenge its descendants even today to a greater loyalty to biblical teachings.

Thieleman J. van Braght collected the accounts of martyrdom with hope that they would inspire the reader to hold as steadfastly to the faith as did the martyrs of whom he wrote.

❸ "Menno's Conversion, Call and Testimony.,"
In his reply to Gellius Faber, Menno Simons candidly shares his faith journey from priest to a hunted Anabaptist preacher. Menno's personal conversion and renewal helped perpetuate the Radical Reformation and twenty-first-century Mennonites are beneficiaries of his passionate ministry and leadership. Menno's account of his conversion, call, and testimony can be found in *The Complete Writings of Menno Simons* (Herald Press, 1956).

❹ "The Anabaptist Vision"

By the twentieth century, most historians viewed sixteenth-century Anabaptists as fringe radicals who made little contribution to mainstream Christianity. Mennonites were trying to decide what it meant to be a Mennonite—were they modernists or fundamentalists? What did their faith say about how to respond to World War II? In 1943 Mennonite leader Harold S. Bender became president of the American Society of Church History. His presidential address, which was reprinted and widely distributed among Mennonites inspired a generation of Mennonites by clarifying that Anabaptism was a distinct and biblical third option to the social debates of the times.

❺ *The Politics of Jesus*

Written by Mennonite theologian John Howard Yoder, *The Politics of Jesus* (Eerdmans, 1972) introduced evangelical Christians to the ethical implications of the life and teachings of Jesus. He demonstrated that the gospel of Jesus Christ is not to be relegated only to a future spiritual realm but begins here and now. *The Politics of Jesus* has been reissued in a second edition and translated into many different languages.

FOUR IMPORTANT THINGS EARLY MENNONITES SAID

❶ Concerning an Active Faith

"For true evangelical faith is of such a nature that it cannot lie dormant, but manifests itself in all righteousness and works of love; it dies unto the flesh and blood; it destroys all forbidden lusts and desires; it seeks and serves and fears God; it clothes the naked; it feeds the hungry; it comforts the sorrowful; it shelters the destitute; it aides and consoles the sad; it returns good for evil; it serves those that harm it; it prays for those that persecute it; teaches, admonishes, and reproves with the Word of the Lord; it seeks that which is lost; it binds up that which is wounded; it heals that which is diseased and it saves that which is sound; it has become all things to all men."

—Menno Simons, *Complete Writings*, 1539

❷ Concerning Nonviolence

"Our weapons are not weapons with which cities and countries may be destroyed, wall and gates broken down, and human blood shed in torrents like water. But they are weapons with which the spiritual kingdom of the devil is destroyed and the wicked principle in man's soul is broken down, flinty hearts broken, hearts that have never been sprinkled with the heavenly dew of the Holy Word. We have and know no other weapons besides this, the Lord knows. . . . Once more, Christ is our fortress; patience our weapon of defense; the Word of God our sword; and our victory a courageous, firm, unfeigned faith in Jesus Christ."

—Menno Simons, "Foundation," 1539

Hans Denck's words have been an inspiration to many.

No one can follow Christ

③ Concerning Wealth, Prosperity, Apathy, and Faith
"When our hearts were golden our houses were wooden, when our houses became golden our hearts became wooden."
—unknown Dutch Mennonite pastor, c. 1670s

④ Concerning the Nature of Faith
"No one may truly know Christ, except one follow him in life, and no one may follow Christ unless he had first known him. Whoever does not know him does not have him and without him he cannot come to the Father. But whoever knows him and does not witness to him by his life will be judged by him. . . . For whoever thinks he belongs to Christ must walk the way that Christ walked."
—Hans Denck, "The Contention that Scripture Says," 1526

HISTORY'S MOST NOTORIOUS HERETICS

❶ The Anabaptists

The people who joined the grassroots movement that was birthed during the Reformation in Europe in the sixteenth century were eventually given the name Anabaptists, or "re-baptizers." This group of Christians believed in adult baptism and refused to baptize their babies into the Catholic church. They did not believe in war or killing of any kind. For these practices, the Anabaptists were ruthlessly persecuted by both the Catholics and the newly established Protestants. Thousands were drowned, burned at the stake, and tortured in various ways.

Anneken Hendriks burned at Amsterdam in 1571 by Jan Luyken.

FIVE THINGS YOU SHOULD KNOW ABOUT THE ANABAPTIST REFORMATION

❶ Johannes Gutenberg invented the first printing press in 1447.

During the century before the Reformation, printing made it possible for more Bibles to be read by the common people. Instead of viewing drawings and painted glass windows, people increasingly read printed works. Knowledge came closer to the hands of the people because printed books could be sold for a fraction of the cost of earlier illuminated manuscripts. More copies of each book became available, people could discuss them, and new movements flourished.

❷ The "Anabaptist" reformers were Catholic.

Most of the earliest reformers wanted to make changes within the one Christian church in Europe, but they wanted to stay Catholic. None of them ever expected that their actions would lead to the dozens of Christian denominations around today.

❸ People in medieval times weren't allowed to choose their own religion.

You could believe whatever you wanted, but you could only practice the faith your prince or king chose. Not to participate in the state church was illegal and punishable by death.

❹ The Anabaptists weren't the only reformers.

Change and ferment were in the air. Beginning with Martin Luther and including many now famous names, numerous reformers wanted the church to rediscover the good news of Jesus that creates and restores faith. Some of the hotly debated topics were separation of church and state, a mystical relationship with God, better-educated priests, and more moral leaders in the church.

5 **Anabaptist reformers cared deeply about adult baptism and social justice.**

Anabaptists got their name for being baptized on confession of faith and commitment to Jesus Christ and the church. During a time when children were baptized as infants, adult baptisms were re-baptisms. Peasant unrest and reform was tied to the Anabaptist reformation in many ways. They took Jesus' words literally and preached a gospel of liberation and jubilee, but also of peace.

FIVE FACTS ABOUT LIFE IN MEDIEVAL TIMES

1 **It lasted more than 1,000 years.**
By some counts, the medieval period (or Middle Ages) covered an era that began around the year 391 (when Christianity became the Roman Empire's only legal religion) and ended around 1517 (the year Martin Luther wrote the Ninety-five Theses).

2 **Life was nasty, brutish, and short.**
People who survived childhood usually did not live long past age 40. If disease or starvation didn't get you, violence and warfare did. It's been estimated that during the 1400s about one-third of Europe's population died of bubonic plague. Sanitation was practically non existent.

Road travel was harsh and sanitation was minimal during the Middle Ages.

❸ The Christian church grew larger, more influential, and more dominant.

Headquartered in Rome, the Western church became a superpower. Church and state became inseparable. At its height (ca. 1000–1300), "Christian Crusaders" battled with Muslims and others for control of the "Holy Land," Thomas Aquinas wrote his *Summa Theologica*, and hundreds of "heretics" were burned to death.

❹ The Christian church grew economically oppressive.

Over the centuries, the church acquired large estates of land and often managed it with the same indifference and exploitation toward the people working the land as the secular nobility. They also developed a "Cult of the Saints" by which the leftover good works (merits) of the saints could be distributed to others, with the pope in charge of this store (treasury) of good works. The early Mennonites spoke out against these injustices.

❺ Humanist and Renaissance-age thinkers also worked for reform.

At the end of the Middle Ages, early reformers such as Jan Hus and Girolamo Savonarola confronted the church corruptions they saw. Hus was burned, and Savonarola was hanged.

THE MENNONITE FAMILY IN NORTH AMERICA

The first Mennonites arrived in North America in 1683 and have since spread to every province of Canada and almost every state in the USA. The two largest conferences, Mennonite Church USA and Mennonite Church Canada, have a combined membership of about 150,000.

Two related groups are the Amish, who live in traditional communities mainly in Pennsylvania, Indiana, and Ohio, and the Hutterites, who live on large communal farms in the prairie states, mainly Manitoba, Alberta, Montana, and South Dakota.

Brethren church groups also came from Anabaptist roots and include Church of the Brethren, Brethren Church, and Grace Brethren.

Today there are 1.4 million Mennonites around the world and 458,000 in the USA and Canada. The main North American Mennonite conferences or Anabaptist church groups (adult members only) are listed below.

Amish	116,000
Beachy Amish Mennonite	8,000
Brethren in Christ	24,000
Church of God in Christ (Holdeman)	18,000
Conservative Mennonite Conference	11,000
Hutterian Brethren	16,000
Mennonite Brethren Church	64,000
Mennonite Church Canada	34,000
Mennonite Church USA	111,000
Old Order Mennonites	22,000
Other Mennonites	34,000

WORLD RELIGIONS

Listed by approximate number of adherents:

Christianity	2 billion
Islam	1.3 billion
Hinduism	900 million
Agnostic/Atheist/Non-Religious	850 million
Buddhism	360 million
Confucianism and Chinese traditional	225 million
Primal-indigenous	150 million
Shinto	108 million
African traditional	95 million
Sikhism	23 million
Juche	19 million
Judaism	14 million
Spiritism	14 million
Baha'i	7 million
Jainism	4 million
Cao Dai	3 million
Tenrikyo	2.4 million
Neo-Paganism	1 million
Unitarian-Universalism	800,000
Rastafarianism	700,000
Scientology	600,000
Zoroastrianism	150,000

COMPARATIVE RELIGIONS

	Baha'i	Buddhism	Christianity
Founder and date founded	Bahá'u'lláh (1817-1892) founded Babism in 1844 from which Baha'i grew.	Founded by Siddhartha Gautama (the Buddha) in Nepal in the 6th-5th centuries BC.	Founded by Jesus of Nazareth, a Palestinian Jew, in the early 1st century AD.
Number of adherents in 2000	About 7 million worldwide; 750,000 U.S.	360 million worldwide; 2 million U.S.	About 2 billion worldwide; 160 million U.S.
Main tenets	The oneness of God, the oneness of humanity, and the common foundation of all religion. Also, equality of men and women, universal education, world peace, and a world federal government.	Meditation and the practice of virtuous and moral behavior can lead to Nirvana, the state of enlightenment. Before that, one is subjected to repeated lifetimes, based on behavior.	Jesus is the Son of God and God in human form. In his death and resurrection, he redeems humanity from sin and gives believers eternal life. His teachings frame the godly life for his followers.
Sacred or primary writing	Bahá'u'lláh's teachings, along with those of the Bab, are collected and published	The Buddha's teachings and wisdom are collected and published.	The Bible is a collection of Jewish and Near Eastern writings spanning some 1,400 years.

Confucianism	Hinduism	Islam	Judaism
Founded by the Chinese philosopher Confucius in the 6th-5th centuries BC. One of several traditional Chinese religions.	Developed in the 2nd century BC from indigenous religions in India, and later combined with other religions, such as Vaishnavism.	Founded by the prophet Muhammad ca. AD 610. The word Islam is Arabic for "submission to God."	Founded by Abraham, Isaac, and Jacob ca. 2000 BC.
6 million worldwide (does not include other traditional Chinese beliefs); U.S. uncertain.	900 million worldwide; 950,000 U.S.	1.3 billion worldwide; 5.6 million U.S	14 million worldwide; 5.5 million U.S.
Confucius's followers wrote down his sayings or Analects. They stress relationships between individuals, families, and society based on proper behavior and sympathy.	Hinduism is based on a broad system of sects. The goal is release from repeated reincarnation through yoga, adherence to the Vedic scriptures, and devotion to a personal guru.	Followers worship Allah through the Five Pillars. Muslims who die believing in God, and that Muhammad is God's messenger, will enter Paradise.	Judaism holds the belief in a monotheistic God, whose Word is revealed in the Hebrew Bible, especially the Torah. Jews await the coming of a messiah to restore creation.
Confucius's Analects are collected and still published.	The Hindu scriptures and Vedic texts.	The Qur'an is a collection of Muhammad's writings.	The Hebrew scriptures compose the Christian Old Testament, with some additional material.

FAMILY TREE OF CHRISTIANITY

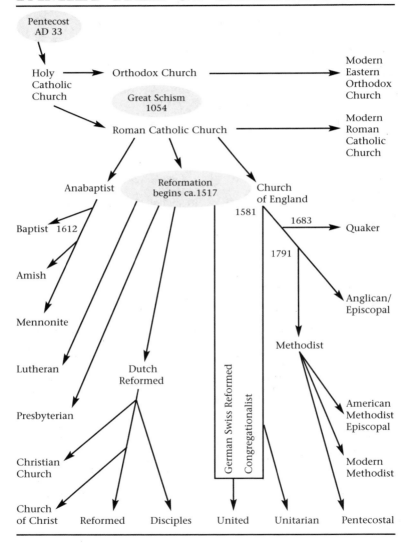

CHRISTIAN DENOMINATIONS IN THE USA AND CANADA

Listed by approximate number of adult adherents:

Catholic	68 million
Baptist	35 million
Methodist/Wesleyan	10 million
Lutheran	10 million
Orthodox	6 million
Presbyterian	5 million
Episcopalian/Anglican	4 million
Pentecostal/Charismatic	3 million
Assemblies of God	3 million
Congregational/ United Church of Christ	2.5 million
Churches of Christ	2 million
Adventist	936,000
Anabaptist Mennonite	458,000
Brethren	167,000

COMPARATIVE DENOMINATIONS:

	Lutheran	Catholic	Orthodox
Founded when and by whom?	1517: Martin Luther challenges Catholic teachings with his Ninety-five Theses. 1530: the Augsburg Confession is published.	Catholics consider Jesus' disciple Peter (died ca. AD 66) the first pope. Through Gregory the Great (540-604), papacy is firmly established.	AD 330: Emperor Constantine renames Byzantium "Constantinople" and declares Christianity the empire's religion.
Adherents in 2000?	About 60 million worldwide; about 9 million U.S.	About 1 billion worldwide; 60 million U.S.	About 225 million worldwide; about 4 million U.S.
How is Scripture viewed?	Protestant canon contains 39 OT books, 27 NT. Scripture alone is the authoritative witness to the gospel.	The canon is 46 books in the OT (Apocryhpha included) and 27 in the NT. Interpretation is subject to church tradition.	49 OT books (Catholic plus three more) and 27 NT. Scripture is subject to tradition.
How are we saved?	We are saved by grace when God grants righteousness through faith alone. Good works inevitably result, but they are not the basis of salvation.	God infuses the gift of faith in the baptized, which is maintained by good works and receiving Penance and the Eucharist.	God became human so humans could be deified, that is, have the energy of God's life in them.
What is the church?	The congregation of believers, mixed with the lost, in which the gospel is preached and the sacraments are administered.	The mystical body of Christ, who established it with the pope as its head; he pronounces doctrine infallibly.	The body of Christ in unbroken historical connection with the apostles; the Roman pope is one of many patriarchs who govern.
What about the sacraments?	Baptism is necessary for salvation. The Lord's Supper is bread & wine that, with God's Word are truly Jesus' body & blood.	Catholics hold seven sacraments. Baptism removes original sin; usually infants. The Eucharist undergoes transubstantiation.	Baptism initiates God's life in the baptized; adults and children. In the Eucharist, bread & wine are changed into body & blood.

Liturgical Churches

	Anglican	Presbyterian	Methodist
Founded when and by whom?	Henry VIII is declared head of the Church of England. 1549: Thomas Cranmer produces the first *Book of Common Prayer*.	1536: John Calvin writes *Institutes of the Christian Religion*. 1789: Presbyterian Church U.S.A. is organized.	1738: Anglican ministers John and Charles Wesley convert. 1784: U.S. Methodists form a separate church body.
Adherents in 2000?	45-75 million worldwide; about 3 million U.S.	40-48 million worldwide; 4 million U.S.	20-40 million worldwide; about 13 million U.S.
How is Scripture viewed?	Protestant canon accepted. Scripture is interpreted in light of tradition and reason.	Protestant canon accepted. Scripture is "witness without parallel" to Christ, but in human words reflecting beliefs of the time.	Protestant canon accepted. Scripture is primary source for Christian doctrine.
How are we saved?	We share in Christ's victory, who died for our sins, freeing us through baptism to become living members of the church.	We are saved by grace alone. Good works result, but are not the basis of salvation.	We are saved by grace alone. Good works must result, but do not obtain salvation.
What is the church?	The body of Christ is based on "apostolic succession" of bishops, going back to the apostles. In the U.S., it is the Episcopal Church.	The body of Christ includes all of God's chosen and is represented by the visible church. Governed by regional "presbyteries" of elders.	The body of Christ, represented by church institutions. Bishops oversee regions and appoint pastors, who are itinerant.
What about the sacraments?	Baptism brings infant and convert initiates into the church; in Communion, Christ's body & blood are truly present.	Baptism is not necessary for salvation. The Lord's Supper is Christ's body & blood, which are spiritually present to believers.	Baptism is a sign of regeneration; in the Lord's Supper, Jesus is really present.

COMPARATIVE DENOMINATIONS:

	Anabaptist	Congregational	Baptist
Founded when and by whom?	1525: Protestants in Zurich, Switzerland, begin believers' baptism. 1536: Menno Simons begins Mennonite movement.	1607: Members of England's illegal "house church" exiled. 1620: Congregationalists arrive in the New World on the Mayflower.	1612: John Smythe and other Puritans form the first Baptist church. 1639: The first Baptist church in America is established.
Adherents in 2000?	About 1.4 million worldwide; about 450,000 U.S. and Canada	More than 2 million worldwide; about 2 million U.S.	100 million worldwide; about 30 million U.S.
How is Scripture viewed?	Protestant canon accepted. Scripture is inspired, fully reliable and trustworthy. Jesus is living Word; Scripture is written Word.	Protestant canon accepted. Bible is the authoritative witness to the Word of God.	Protestant canon accepted. Scripture is inspired and without error; the sole rule of faith.
How are we saved?	Salvation is a personal experience. Through faith in Jesus, we become at peace with God, moving us to follow Jesus' example by being peacemakers.	God promises forgiveness and grace to save "from sin and aimlessness" all who trust him, who accept his call to serve the whole human family.	Salvation is offered freely to all who accept Jesus as Savior. There is no salvation apart from personal faith in Christ.
What is the church?	The body of Christ, the assembly and society of believers. No one system of government is recognized.	The people of God living as Jesus' disciples. Each local church is self-governing and chooses its own ministers.	The body of Christ; the redeemed throughout history. The term church usually refers to local congregations, which are autonomous.
What about the sacraments?	Baptism is for believers only. The Lord's Supper is a memorial of his death.	Congregations may practice infant baptism or believers' baptism or both. Sacraments are symbols.	Baptism is immersion of believers, only as a symbol. The Lord's Supper is symbolic

Non-Liturgical Churches

	Churches of Christ	Adventist	Pentecostal
Founded when and by whom?	1801: Barton Stone holds Cane Ridge Revival in Kentucky. 1832: Stone's Christians unite with Disciples of Christ.	1844: William Miller's prediction of Christ's return that year failed. 1863: Seventh-Day Adventist Church is organized.	1901: Kansas college students speak in tongues. 1906: Azusa Street revival in L.A. launches movement. 1914: Assemblies of God organized.
Adherents in 2000?	5-6 million worldwide; about 3 million U.S.	About 11 million worldwide; about 100,000 U.S.	About 500 million worldwide; about 5 million U.S.
How is Scripture viewed?	Protestant canon accepted. Scripture is the Word of God. Disciples of Christ view it as a witness to Christ, but fallible.	Protestant canon accepted. Scripture is inspired and without error; Ellen G. White, an early leader, was a prophet.	Protestant canon accepted. Scripture is inspired and without error. Some leaders are considered prophets.
How are we saved?	We must hear the gospel, repent, confess Christ, and be baptized. Disciples of Christ: God saves people by grace.	We repent by believing in Christ as Example (in his life) and Substitute (by his death). Those who are found right with God will be saved.	We are saved by God's grace through Jesus, resulting in our being born again in the Spirit, as evidenced by a life of holiness.
What is the church?	The assembly of those who have responded rightly to the gospel; it must be called only by the name of Christ.	Includes all who believe in Christ. The last days are a time of apostasy, when a remnant keeps God's commandments faithfully.	The body of Christ, in which the Holy Spirit dwells; the agency for bringing the gospel of salvation to the whole world.
What about the sacraments?	Baptism is the immersion of believers only, as the initial act of obedience to the gospel. The Lord's Supper is a symbolic memorial.	Baptism is the immersion of believers only. Baptism and the Lord's Supper are symbolic only.	Baptism is immersion of believers only. A further "baptism in the Holy Spirit" is offered. Lord's Supper is symbolic.

THE SEASONS OF THE CHURCH YEAR AND WHAT THEY MEAN

Advent is a season of longing and anticipation, during which we prepare for the coming of Jesus. The church year begins with Advent, as life begins with birth, starting four Sundays before Christmas.

Christmas is a day and a season when we celebrate God's coming among us as a human child: Jesus, Emmanuel (which means "God with us"). Christmas lasts for 12 days, from December 25 to January 5.

Epiphany is celebrated on January 6, when we remember the Magi's visit to the Christ child. During the time after Epiphany we hear stories about Jesus' baptism and early ministry.

Lent is a season when we turn toward God and think about how our lives need to change. This is also a time to remember our baptism and how that gift gives us a new start every day! Lent begins on Ash Wednesday and lasts for 40 days (not including Sundays) and ends on the Saturday before Easter Sunday.

The Three Days are the most important part of the Christian calendar because they mark Jesus' last days, death, and resurrection. These days (approximately three 24-hour periods) begin on Maundy Thursday evening and conclude on Easter evening. On Maundy Thursday we hear the story of Jesus' last meal with his disciples and his act of service and love in washing their feet. On Good Friday we hear of Jesus' trial, crucifixion, death, and burial. On Saturday, at the nighttime Easter Vigil, we hear stories about the amazing things God has done for us. It is a night of light, Scripture readings, baptismal remembrance, and communion—the greatest night of the year for Christians. On Easter Sunday we celebrate Jesus' resurrection and our new lives in Christ. Easter falls on a different date each year—sometime between March 22 and April 25.

Easter is not just one day, but a whole season when we celebrate the resurrected Jesus. The season begins on Easter Sunday and lasts for 50 days (including Sundays). The Day of Pentecost falls on the 50th day of the season (Pentecost means 50th), when we honor the Holy Spirit and the church's mission in the world.

Time after Pentecost is the longest season in the church calendar, lasting almost half the year. Sometimes this is called "ordinary time" because there aren't many special celebrations during these weeks.

THE SEASONS OF THE CHURCH YEAR

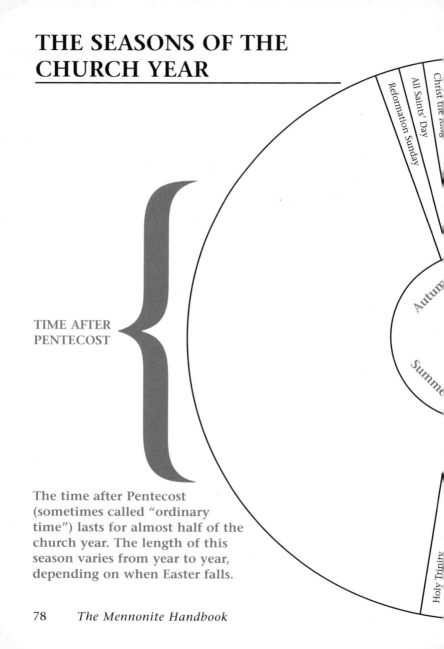

Christ the King

All Saints' Day

Reformation Sunday

Autumn

Summer

Holy Trinity

TIME AFTER PENTECOST

The time after Pentecost (sometimes called "ordinary time") lasts for almost half of the church year. The length of this season varies from year to year, depending on when Easter falls.

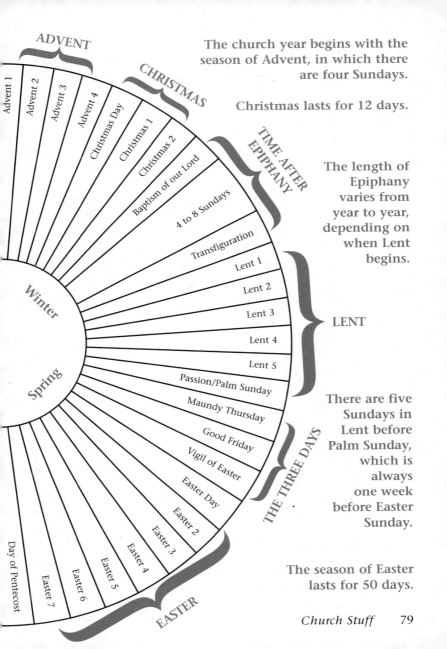

The church year begins with the season of Advent, in which there are four Sundays.

Christmas lasts for 12 days.

The length of Epiphany varies from year to year, depending on when Lent begins.

There are five Sundays in Lent before Palm Sunday, which is always one week before Easter Sunday.

The season of Easter lasts for 50 days.

ADVENT
Advent 1
Advent 2
Advent 3
Advent 4

CHRISTMAS
Christmas Day
Christmas 1
Christmas 2
Baptism of our Lord

TIME AFTER EPIPHANY
4 to 8 Sundays
Transfiguration

LENT
Lent 1
Lent 2
Lent 3
Lent 4
Lent 5
Passion/Palm Sunday
Maundy Thursday

THE THREE DAYS
Good Friday
Vigil of Easter

EASTER
Easter Day
Easter 2
Easter 3
Easter 4
Easter 5
Easter 6
Easter 7
Day of Pentecost

Winter

Spring

MENNO SIMONS

After much soul searching, the 40-year-old priest, Menno Simons, cast his lot with the Anabaptists. Menno Simons (1496-1561) spent the rest of his life as a fugitive, writer, and traveling pastor among the scattered and persecuted Anabaptist fellowships.

ANABAPTIST EUROPE

Anabaptism sprang up in various parts of Europe during the 16th century. Menno Simons led the movement in the Netherlands, while Felix Manz and Conrad Grebel were early leaders in Switzerland.

EVERYDAY STUFF

Believing in God involves more than going to church and reading the Bible. It's about keeping your faith with you in every part of your life.

This section includes:

- Advice for helping people in times of trouble.

- Tips on forgiving others and treating them with respect—even if you don't always feel like it.

- Top ten things to look for in a spouse.

HOW TO SHARE YOUR FAITH WITH SOMEONE

Sharing the gospel with others is a natural part of exercising a mature faith. In fact, Jesus commanded his followers to do this, making it an important part of the life of faith (Matthew 28:18-20). While *evangelism* has become a negative word for some people, sharing the story of salvation in Jesus Christ is still the most rewarding way to live out one's faith. It is also a discipline that takes practice.

1 **Remember there are different ways to be an evangelist.** St. Francis of Assisi said, "Preach the gospel daily and use words if you have to." Mennonites sometimes feel more comfortable cooking a meal or swinging a hammer instead of talking. These are also valid translations of the gospel message. See Menno Simons' quote on true evangelical faith, page 59.

2 **Look for the opening.** Regular daily conversations offer lots of chances to talk about your faith. Listen for open-ended comments, such as, "I wonder why life is like that," or, "Sometimes life seems so hard." When possible, offer a response from a Christian perspective. Begin sentences with phrases such as, "I've come to think . . ." or, "I don't have the perfect answer, but I believe . . . "

3 **Be yourself.** Expressing your faith should be natural and the same as other types of daily conversation. Avoid suddenly switching your tone of voice or vocabulary. Also, don't try to impress the other person with your knowledge. Allow the Holy Spirit to guide you.

4 Watch for a chance to take the conversation deeper.
Carefully gauge the other person's response. Observe his or
her facial expression, verbal tone, and body language. If he
or she seems to be closing down, set the topic aside and
wait for another time. If he or she keys in and perks up, be
prepared to continue.

5 Open up.
Human beings are attracted to each other by our strengths,
but we bond because of our weaknesses. Key to sharing
your faith is the willingness to be honest about your own
life's struggles. This will communicate safety, which for
many people is critical.

6 Follow up.
Offer to continue the conversation later and arrange a time.
At this point, the conversation will have become personally
valuable to you. Allowing the person to see your commitment
to your faith alongside your continuing questions will
reassure him or her of your sincerity.

7 Offer to share your faith community with the other person.
Most people join a church after being invited by a friend.
When the time is right, invite the person to attend with
you. Tell the person what makes it special to you.

8 Try to maintain the relationship regardless of what the
person does.
Be prepared for the other person to shut down around faith
talk, decline your invitation to attend church, or even appear
to avoid you. The most effective way to communicate that
you're a follower of Jesus Christ is through your actions;
continue to live naturally and with integrity.

HOW TO HANDLE MISTAKEN IDENTITY

As a Mennonite it is not uncommon to be confused with our more famous spiritual siblings, the Amish or the Hutterites. Someone may learn that you are a Mennonite and ask something such as "Oh, did you get here in a buggy?" "Do you have electricity at home?" or [to women] "Don't you wear dresses?" These questions are generally well-meaning although they can catch you off guard and cause uncomfortable feelings. The goal is to inform as well as, if possible, plant a seed that will inspire your acquaintance to learn more about your church and faith in general.

❶ Remain calm.
Talking about your faith, especially with a stranger can be stressful and uncomfortable. Take a few deep breaths and say a quick prayer that God would give you the words to say.

❷ Don't become defensive.
Your friend is probably simply intrigued; don't feel the need to defend yourself or Mennonitism at large, though giving good facts is important in educating your friend.

❸ Don't trash others.
Regardless of your opinions concerning the Amish, Hutterites, Old Order and Old Colony Mennonites, or anyone else you may be confused with, this is not the time to vent. While it may be tempting to disparage others to make yourself look better, don't—this generally has quite the opposite effect.

❹ Know your facts and history.

• Old Order Mennonites dress plain and drive buggies, so your questioner is not completely off base. Keep your history lesson short and to the point. If someone assumes you are:

• Amish—"The Amish and Mennonites are both part of the Anabaptist movement that started in Reformation times. However, we split over church discipline differences in 1693 back in Europe. The Amish have held to a stricter discipline on issues such as dress and technology than the Mennonites. Many Mennonites today are impossible to pick out of a crowd."

• Hutterite—"The Hutterites and Mennonites are both part of the Anabaptist movement that started in Reformation times. However, beginning in 1528, one group of Anabaptists decided to live in community and share their possessions in common. Jakob Hutter, a prominent Anabaptist leader and preacher, became an important leader with this group a few years later. The Hutterites practice common possession of goods to this day, living in colonies mainly in Alberta, Manitoba, and Saskatchawan."

• A more conservative Mennonite group—"The Mennonite church's roots go back to the Anabaptist movement during Reformation times in the 1500s. Since then there have been many divisions based on biblical interpretation and church discipline. We share a name and the same basic Christian beliefs, however."

❺ Know your theology.

A truly curious person may ask, "So what are Mennonites?" And you want to be ready for this opportunity. There is much one could say (see Mennonite Stuff, pages 177-203), but this is a suggestion: "Mennonites grew out of the

Anabaptist movement during Protestant Reformation times and share beliefs similar to other Christian denominations with roots in that period, including the Lutheran and Reformed churches. However, Mennonites emphasize pacifism, believer's baptism, strong community, and family values."

Be Aware

• Mennonites, as a small, more unknown denomination get confused with a variety of religious beliefs. On a Saturday someone may ask you why you aren't in church, or they may confuse you for a Mormon because they both start with M. It happens. Follow the steps above, making the necessary adjustments, and pray that God would use your conversation for the work of the church

• You may need to define such terms as Reformation, believer's baptism, and pacifism. Be prepared (reading pages 177-204 several times will be a good start).

HOW TO PRAY

Prayer is intimate communication with God and can be used before a meal, at bedtime, during a worship service, or any time the need or opportunity arises. Silent and spoken prayers are both okay and may be used liberally throughout the day. Prayer is also taking time to listen to what God is saying to us. Spontaneous prayer is often best, but the following process may help build the habit.

❶ **Assess your need for prayer.**
Take stock of the situation at hand, including your motivations. What are you praying for and why?

❷ **Select a type of prayer.**
Prayers of supplication (requests for God's help), contrition (in which sin is confessed and forgiveness requested), intercession (on behalf of others), and others are good and time tested. Books of personal prayers, hymnals, and devotionals often contain helpful, prewritten prayers. Consider also an ad-lib prayer from the heart.

❸ **Select a physical prayer posture.**
Many postures are appropriate:

• The most common type of prayer in the New Testament is from a prone position, lying face-down on the ground, arms spread.

• Kneeling with your face and palms upturned is good for prayers of supplication.

• Bowed head with closed eyes and hands folded is common today and aids concentration.

There is no "official" posture for prayer. Choose your posture according to your individual prayer needs.

❹ Offer your prayer.
Pray with confidence. God listens to all prayer and responds. Breathe deeply, relax, and be open as the Spirit leads you.

❺ Listen.
Take time during your prayer simply to listen. Some prayer traditions involve only silent meditation as a means of listening for God's voice.

Choose a comfortable and appropriate prayer posture for your prayer time.

Be Aware

• God hears every prayer.

• Prayer can be done either alone or in the company of others (corporately).

• Environment matters. If possible, consider lighting a candle and dimming the lights to set the mood and help block out distractions.

HOW TO WORK FOR PEACE AND JUSTICE ON BEHALF OF PEOPLE WHO ARE POOR AND OPPRESSED

Knowing that good works are the result—not the cause—of salvation, Mennonites have a long record of working for physical and economic justice, relief, and development around the world. For example, Mennonite Central Committee is a respected, efficient, and effective aid organization.

Mennonite congregations around the globe also set justice as one of their highest priorities, giving time and money both locally and globally. As followers of Jesus Christ, each individual Christian is linked to Jesus' compassion for people who are poor and marginalized and called to work tirelessly on their behalf, as he did.

❶ Include people who are poor and oppressed in your daily prayers.
Keeping the needs of others in mind, especially people who suffer as a result of economic inequality, political oppression, or natural disaster, defines a person's good works. Name specific situations in your prayers, and use specific place names and people's names whenever possible. Keep the newspaper on your lap as you pray if necessary.

❷ Include people who are poor and oppressed in your personal or household budget.
Dedicate some of your personal giving to economic-aid organizations. This should include people in your congregation. If you already tithe (give 10 percent of your income to

your church), consider earmarking a percentage of that money to go directly to relief organizations through your church's budget. Be creative, for example, consider matching every dollar that you spend on pet food with a dollar toward relieving human hunger.

❸ Pay close attention to economic and political conditions in other nations.
You can't help if you don't know what's really going on. Resolve to be a well-informed person who tests the worldview in the news against the worldview in the Bible. Utilize the Internet to locate independent and alternative news sources with unique, on-the-spot perspectives.

❹ Get to know organizations that work for justice locally.
Your congregation probably already organizes to do justice work in your neighborhood. If not, consider taking responsibility to organize a ministry team in your church.

❺ Make working for justice part of your weekly or monthly routine.
Devote a portion of your time regularly to a specific activity that personally connects you to people who are poor and disenfranchised. There is no substitute for personal contact.

❻ Advocate for a cause in which you believe, one that has meaning for you personally.
The best way to get involved and stay involved is through a cause that you can be truly passionate about. Resist the temptation to jump on the nearest bandwagon.

7 Live justly in your personal economic life.

In North America the consumer has real power. Make a point to ask your grocery stores, coffee shops, stockbroker, favorite clothing stores, and other vendors how and from where they get their products. Let them know that as a consumer it matters where your money goes. You will most likely spend more money for fairly traded, environmentally friendly, labor-conscious, taint-free products, so be prepared. Look at your budget and decide to consume less, but more responsibly.

HOW TO BE A PACIFIST

Mennonites believe that pacifism and nonresistance are central to the gospel message and confess that this is the biblical way to live. They have many stories of refusing military service or seeking alternatives to violence. Pacifism is not easy, but then again, not many important things are.

❶ Recognize that peace is the will of God.
God created humans to live in peace, and the Garden of Eden contained no violence or death. God sent Jesus to reveal God's full and perfect peace. It is humans who have chosen violence and injustice, not God.

❷ Learn from Jesus' nonresistant response to evil (Matthew 23:1-36).
Jesus confronted injustice, hypocrisy, and oppression, but he did it in nonviolent ways. Ultimately he accepted torture and crucifixion on the cross, offering forgiveness and love to his enemies. His life and his teachings show us that peace and justice are not optional teachings that Christians can take or leave.

❸ Ask the Spirit to empower you.
The same Spirit that came to Jesus in the Garden of Gethsemane is able to empower you to love enemies, to forgive rather than to seek revenge, to practice right relationships, and to resist evil without violence.

❹ Be proactive in your peace making.
A pacifist does not just react peaceably to violence but actively works to prevent it: in speech, in relationships, in economic matters, in relief work, in all ways. Many mediation and restorative justice workshops are offered by churches, schools, and conferences; enroll in one.

HOW TO IDENTIFY A GENUINE MIRACLE

The term miracle describes something that causes wonder. It is usually used in reference to an event that defies logical explanation and appears to be the work of a higher force, suggesting a reality beyond the five senses.

❶ Disregard most minor situations.
The facts should indicate a situation of high order, such as one that is life threatening, causes suffering, or involves an immediate threat. Finding your lost keys does not necessarily constitute a miracle.

❷ Look for a lack of predictability.
A positive outcome should be needed and wanted, but not expected. Miracles tend to occur "out of the blue" rather than as the result of an earthly cause, especially a human one.

❸ Evaluate the outcome.
Miracles achieve a life-giving purpose; they never occur outside the will of God. Suffering is relieved, God is glorified, Jesus' presence is made manifest, the lowly are lifted up, evil is thwarted, creation is revealed, or life is saved. The outcome must be regarded as good, according to biblical standards (compare with the fruits of the Spirit, Galatians 5:22).

❹ Look for a divine agency.
The ability to make a miracle happen, to guarantee the results, or to take credit for it is beyond human. Often the event will defy what we know to be true about the laws of nature or probability. If anyone stands to make money or advance an agenda from an event, it is most likely not a miracle.

5 Adopt a wait-and-see perspective.
A miracle will still be a miracle later on. Labeling something a miracle too quickly could lead down unhelpful paths, while waiting to make the call—pondering the event in your heart—will enhance your faith journey.

Be Aware

• The most overlooked miracle is that God shows up in everyday life events and in such ordinary forms as bread, wine, water, words, and people.

• The miracle of life in Jesus Christ is a daily event and should be regarded as a free gift.

THREE ESSENTIAL PERSONAL SPIRITUAL RITUALS

A spiritual ritual is a routine for building one's faith. Ritual involves action, words, and often images that work together to center one's daily life in Jesus Christ. Medical studies show that people who pray regularly throughout the day suffer less stress, have lower incidence of heart disease, and live longer on average than those who do not.

❶ Morning Devotions

• Directly upon awakening, turn your attention first to God. The silence and solitude available in the morning hours are ideal. (See Morning Prayer on page 195.)

• Try to make prayer the first activity of your day. If necessary, set your alarm to sound 15 minutes early to give yourself time.

• Begin with thanks and by remembering God's constant presence.

• Identify events you anticipate in your day and how you feel about them.

• Ask God to provide what you need for the day.

• Pray on behalf of other people. Consider keeping a list of names tucked inside your Bible or devotional book.

Praying before mealtime is a great personal ritual that can be shared with others.

❷ Mealtime Grace

Human beings naturally pause before a meal. Use those moments to give thanks.

• Consider establishing mealtime grace as a household ritual.

• When eating in public, be considerate of others, but do not abandon your ritual.

• Once your meal is assembled and ready to eat, take time before praying to gather your thoughts and call an appropriate prayer to mind.

• Many people pray a rote or memorized prayer at mealtimes. Consider occasionally departing from your regular prayer with an extemporaneous one.

❸ Evening Prayer

The other daily rituals you perform in the evening, like brushing your teeth or letting the cat out, create a natural structure for evening prayer.

• Establish a regular time, such as sunset or bedtime, and commit to it.

• Confess wrongdoing and ask for forgiveness.

• Tell God about the joys and sorrows of the day. Ask for help with the sorrows, and give thanks for the joys.

• Identify the good things about the day. On bad days, find at least one thing to give thanks for.

• Consider using a devotional as a guide and companion. (See Evening Prayer on page 196.)

• Think about involving other members of your household in this ritual. Evening prayer particularly can be enhanced through sharing.

WHY CONFESSING SIN AND RECEIVING FORGIVENESS GO TOGETHER

The Lord's Prayer has a two-sided request concerning forgiveness. We ask God to forgive those who have sinned against us, but *first* we ask forgiveness for our own sins. We cannot dwell on others' missteps until we have dealt with our own (Matthew 7:3-5). This is a continual process.

1 Make a mental list of your offenses.

2 Locate a fellow Christian.
When appropriate, confess your sins to another person.

3 Resolve to confess of your own free will.
Don't confess merely because someone else wants you to do it. Make your confession voluntarily.

4 Make your confession fearlessly, aloud if possible.
Confess the sins that burden you, and then confess the sins of which you are not aware or can't remember.

5 Avoid making up sins.
More important than the facts and figures is a spirit of repentance in your heart.

6 Receive forgiveness as it is given. Resolve to live joyfully and penitently.
God forgives you fully. Rejoice and be glad.

Be Aware

• Unburdening your conscience through confession is cleansing and good for the soul; it's not meant to be torture.

• Ultimately, forgiveness comes from God. To receive forgiveness a perfect and pure confession is not required.

When appropriate, confess your sins to another person.

HOW TO FORGIVE SOMEONE

Forgiving is one of the most difficult disciplines of faith, since it seems to cost you something additional when you've already been wronged. Being a true disciple of Jesus leaves little option, however.

❶ Acknowledge that God forgives you.
When you realize that God has already shown forgiveness and continues to forgive sinners like you, it's easier to forgive someone else.

❷ Consult Scripture.
Jesus taught the Lord's Prayer to his disciples, who were hungry to become like he was. Forgiveness was a big part of this. Read Matthew 6:9-15. Later, when Peter asked how many times he should forgive his brother and suggested that seven may be a good number, Jesus responded, "Not seven times, but seventy-seven times" (Matthew 18:22).

❸ Remember the martyrs.
Jesus called from the cross, "Father, forgive them, for they do not know what they are doing" (Luke 23:34). With these words ringing in their ears, the Anabaptist martyrs of the sixteenth century offered forgiveness to those who tortured them and burned their bodies at the stake. You can do it too.

❹ Seek the person out whenever possible.
Consciously decide to deliver your forgiveness in person. In cases where this is geographically impossible, find an appropriate alternative means, such as the telephone.

Note: This may not be wise in all cases, given the timing of the situation or the level of hurt. Certain problems can be made worse by an unwelcome declaration of forgiveness. Consult with your pastor before taking questionable action.

5 Say, "I forgive you," out loud.
A verbal declaration of forgiveness is ideal. Speaking the words enacts a physical chain reaction that can create healing for both speaker and hearer. In the Bible, Jesus used these words to heal a paralyzed man from across a room.

6 Pray for the power to forgive.
Praying for this is always good, whether a forgiveness situation is at hand or not. It is especially helpful in cases where declaring forgiveness seems beyond your reach.

Be Aware

• When someone sins against you personally, forgiving them does NOT depend upon their feeling sorry (showing contrition) or asking for your forgiveness. But it helps. You may have to struggle, however, to forgive them without their consent or participation.

• The phrase "forgive and forget" is cute, but unhelpful. Even though you truly forgive, you will not always forget. This is normal. When you do remember the offense, simply go through the steps of forgiveness again (remember "not seven times, but seventy-seven").

HOW TO DEFEND YOUR FAITH AGAINST ATTACK

Defending your faith from attack involves tact and savvy, that is, the ability to empathize with your adversary and use his or her affronts creatively without getting baited into an angry or hostile response. The Mennonite theological perspective was hammered out in a context of trial, debate, and mortal danger, though you probably don't need to go looking for a fight nowadays. Just be ready. There is no substitute for knowing your stuff.

❶ Employ the 80/20 rule.
In any debate, it is best to listen at least 80 percent of the time and talk 20 percent of the time.

❷ Engage in empathic listening.
Empathic listening means trying to comprehend not just the content of the other person's position but also the emotional thrust behind it. This is important especially in cases where the speaker's emotional expressions are intense.

❸ Restate your adversary's argument empathetically.
Use sentences like, "So, you're upset because Christians seem to say one thing and do another."

❹ Identify with what the speaker is saying.
For example, say, "I know what you mean. I see a lot of phony behavior at my own church." This elevates the conversation and keeps it civil.

❺ Do your best to put the speaker at ease.
Having made clear that you understand his or her position,

you are free to state your defense or counterpoint. Offer "I statement" responses, such as, "I wonder how I would stand up under that kind of scrutiny myself," or, "I do my best not to judge others too harshly. I'd hate to be judged by those standards."

6 Keep it as upbeat as possible.
Use humility, humor, and a pleasant nature to defuse any tension. Though it is hard to practice, it is possible to disagree with someone while remaining friends.

7 Give your opponent his or her due.
When the speaker makes a good argument, say, "You make a good point." This will further elevate the conversation. If you still disagree, make your counterargument calmly.

8 Avoid closing off the conversation or leaving it on a sour note.
If you can, offer to continue the discussion over a lunch that you buy. Avoid falling into a "winner take all" mind-set. Keep respect as your highest value.

Be Aware

• Attacks on faith are not limited to verbal assaults. In many countries around the world religious persecution is a reality. Take care when visiting such places, especially when distributing religious materials or sharing stories about your faith.

• It is best in all cases to avoid sounding smug or preachy so that your points don't resemble counterattacks.

HOW TO RESIST TEMPTATION

Whether you are a brand new or a mature Christian, temptation is constantly lurking. Ironically, it is usually the small temptations to do wrong that trip us up. Either large or small, we need to be prepared; it is when we are relaxed and confident in our goodness that the devil makes his move.

❶ Run the opposite direction.
Learn to identify the things that tempt you and avoid situations in which temptation will occur. When you see a temptation coming down the road, take a detour.

❷ Laugh at the tempter.
Temptations are simply things that want to gain power over you. When you laugh at them, you reduce them to their proper place.

❸ Distract yourself with other, healthier activities.
God knows what's good for you and so do you. Find an alternate activity that promotes trust in God and requires you to care for your neighbors. Seek the company of others, especially people to whom you may be of service.

❹ Remember, our Lord also confronted temptation.
Jesus faced down temptation by telling the devil the truth, namely, only God is Lord. Consider using a contemporary version of Jesus' words: "God's in charge here, not you."

❺ Tell the devil to go back to hell.
Consider saying this: "You're right, Mr. Devil. I'm a sinner. Unfortunately, you have no power here. My Lord loves sinners and has forgiven me forever. There's nothing you can do about it. Go back to where you came from and quit bothering me!"

Even Jesus faced temptation when the devil confronted him in the wilderness.

Be Aware

- There are different kinds of temptation. Regardless of the type, temptation always involves a hidden voice whispering to you, "Whatever God says, you really need to trust me instead. I'm the only thing that can help you."

- Temptations try to make us trust in ourselves or in other things more than in God. When you realize this, you'll see that everything on the list above is just turning back to Jesus who died to show you how much you can trust him.

- We are often our own worst enemy when it comes to temptation. This is why we need a strong community to help show us where we are weak. Be sure to have friends that aren't afraid to tell it to you straight.

HOW TO CARE FOR THE SICK

While a trained and licensed physician must be sought to treat illness and injury, there is no malady that cannot be helped with faithful attention and prayer.

1 Assess the nature of the problem.
Visit a local pharmacy if the illness is a simple one. Over-the-counter medications usually provide temporary relief until the body heals itself. If symptoms persist, the sick person should see a doctor and get a more detailed diagnosis.

2 Pray for them.
Intercessory prayers are prayers made on someone else's behalf. Recent studies point to healing in hospitalized patients who have been prayed for—even when the sick were not aware of the prayers. Add the afflicted person to your church's prayer list.

3 Call in the elders.
Prayer and emotional support from friends and family are vital parts of healing, living with illness, and facing death. Ask the pastor to assemble the church elders (leaders) for prayer and the laying on of hands.

Here's what the Bible says on this topic: "Are any among you sick? They should call for the elders of the church and have them pray over them, anointing them with oil in the name of the Lord" (James 5:14).

Be Aware

• Many people claim expertise in healing, from acupuncturists and herbalists to "faith healers" and psychics. Use caution and skepticism, but keep an open mind.

• Many people believe that much healing can be found in "comfort foods," such as homemade chicken soup.

• Those who attempt to diagnose and treat their own symptoms can often do more harm than good. When in doubt, always consult a pharmacist, doctor, or other medical professional.

Gather friends, family, and church leaders to pray and lay hands on sick people.

HOW TO IDENTIFY AND AVOID EVIL

The devil delights in unnoticed evil. To this end, the devil employs a wide array of lies, disguises, and deceptions while attacking our relationships with God and each other. A sharp eye and vigilance are your best defense. Mennonites sometimes dislike the subject of evil, but many secretly cultivate extraordinary talent for rooting it out.

1 Know your enemy.
Evil appears in many forms, most often using camouflage to present itself as kindly or friendly. Cruelty, hatred, violence, and exploitation are among the many forms evil can take, but it often masquerades as justice or something done "for their own good." Be alert to acts, people, and events that employ these methods, even if the eventual outcome appears good.

2 Proceed carefully and deliberately.
Avoid rushing to conclusions. Use good judgment.

3 Take action to expose the evil.
Evil relies on darkness. It wants to remain hidden and hates the light of truth. Things that suffer from public knowledge or scrutiny might be evil.

4 Be prepared to make a personal sacrifice.
Fighting evil can be costly. A successful counterattack may require you to give up something you cherish. For Jesus, as for many of his followers, it was his life. Love is the foundation of sacrifice that combats evil.

5 Stay vigilant.
Evil's genius is shown in disguise, deception, and misdirection. Maintain your objectivity and apply the biblical measures of right and wrong you know to be correct. Consult the Scriptures and your church community.

HOW TO AVOID GOSSIP

Gossip is among the most corrosive forces within a community and should be avoided. Discovery of gossip should be viewed as an opportunity to defend your neighbors' integrity, both gossiper and gossipee.

1 Determine whether the conversation at hand qualifies as gossip.
- Gossip involves one party speaking about a second party to a third party.

- The person who is the topic of gossip is not a participant in the conversation.

- The tone of the conversation is often secretive or negative. Gasps and whispers are common.

- The facts expressed in a gossip conversation are often unsubstantiated and have been obtained second- or third-hand.

2 Recall and heed Titus 3:2: "Speak evil of no one."

3 Interject yourself into the conversation politely.
Ask whether the gossiper(s) have spoken directly to the person about whom they are talking. If not, politely ask why. This may give some indication why they are gossiping.

4 Make a statement of fact.
Gossip withers in the face of truth. Make an attempt to find out what is truly known apart from conjecture and supposition. State aloud that gossip is disrespectful and unfair.

5 Offer an alternative explanation based on fact.
Describe other situations that cast the gossipee in a favorable light. Always try to give people the benefit of the doubt.

*Avoid gossip.
It undermines
community
and damages
relationships.*

Be Aware

• There is a fine line between helping and meddling. Pay close attention to your own motivations and the possible outcomes of your actions.

• Gossip injures both the gossiper and the person who is the subject of rumors.

• Church prayer chains can be gossip in the name of "mutual prayer support."

• For further help, consult James 4:11.

HOW TO RESOLVE INTERPERSONAL CONFLICT

Disagreements are part of life. They often occur when we forget that not everyone sees things the same way. Conflict should be viewed as an opportunity to grow, not a contest for domination.

1 Adopt a healthy attitude.
Your frame of mind is critical. Approach the situation with forethought and calm. Prayer can be invaluable at this stage. Do not approach the other party when you're angry or upset.

2 Read Matthew 18:15-20 beforehand.
Consult the Bible to orient your thinking. This is the model Jesus provided and can be used to call to mind an appropriate method.

3 Talk directly to the person involved.
Avoid "triangulation." Talking about someone to a third party can make the conflict worse, since the person may feel that he or she is the subject of gossip. Speaking with the other person directly eliminates the danger and boosts the odds of a good outcome.

4 Express yourself without attacking.
Using "I statements" can avoid casting the other person as the "bad guy" and inflaming the conflict. "I statements" are sentences beginning with phrases such as "I feel . . ." or "I'm uncomfortable when . . ."

5 Keep "speaking the truth in love" (Ephesians 4:15) as your goal.
Your "truth" may not be the other party's. Your objective is to discover and honor each other's "truth," not to put down the other person. Be ready to admit your own faults and mistakes.

6 Seek out a third party to act as an impartial witness.
If direct conversation doesn't resolve the conflict, locate someone both parties trust to sit in. This can help clarify your positions and bring understanding.

7 Build toward forgiveness and a renewed friendship.
Agree upon how you will communicate to prevent future misunderstandings.

Be Aware

• Seemingly unrelated events in your or the other person's life may be playing an invisible role in the conflict at hand. Be ready to shift the focus to the real cause.

• You may not be able to resolve the conflict at this time, but don't give up on future opportunities.

When two people aren't getting along, sometimes an impartial third person can help resolve the dispute.

HOW TO CONSOLE SOMEONE

Consolation is a gift from God. Christians in turn give it to others to build up the body of Christ and preserve it in times of trouble. (See 2 Corinthians 1:4-7.) Mennonites often employ food as a helpful secondary means.

❶ Listen first.
Make it known that you're present and available. When the person opens up, be quiet and attentive.

❷ Be ready to help the person face grief and sadness, not avoid them.
The object is to help the person name, understand, and work through his or her feelings, not gloss over them.

❸ Avoid saying things to make yourself feel better.
"I know exactly how you feel" is seldom true and trivializes the sufferer's pain. Even if you have experienced something similar, no experience is exactly the same. If there is nothing to say, simply be present with the person.

❹ Show respect with honesty.
Don't try to answer the mysteries of the universe or force your beliefs on the person. Be clear about the limitations of your abilities. Be ready to let some questions go unanswered. Consolation isn't about having all the answers, it's about bearing one another's burdens.

❺ Don't put words in God's mouth.
Avoid saying "This is God's will," or "This is part of God's plan." Unless you heard it straight from God, don't say it.

HOW TO COPE
WITH LOSS AND GRIEF

Any loss can cause pain, anger, feelings of confusion, and
uncertainty. These responses are normal.

❶ Familiarize yourself with the stages of grief.
Experts identify five: denial, anger, bargaining, depression,
and acceptance. Some add hope as a sixth stage. Grieving
persons cycle back and forth through the stages, sometimes
experiencing two or three in a single day. This is normal.

❷ Express your grief.
Healthy ways may include crying, staring into space for
extended periods, ruminating, shouting at the ceiling, and
sudden napping. Laughing outbursts are also appropriate
and should not be judged harshly.

❸ Identify someone you trust to talk to.
Available people can include a spouse, parents, relatives,
friends, a pastor, a doctor, or a trained counselor.
Household pets may also make listeners and willing
confidants.

❹ Choose a personal way to memorialize the loss.
Make a collage of photographs, offer a memorial donation
to your church, or start a scrapbook of memories to honor
the event. This helps you to begin to heal without getting
stuck in your grief.

Be Aware

• Many experts prescribe a self-giving activity, such as volunteering at a shelter or soup kitchen, as a means of facilitating a healthy grieving process.

• The pain immediately after suffering a loss is usually deep and intense. This will lessen with the passage of time.

• Anger, guilt, bitterness, and sadness are likely emotions.

• Short-term depression may occur in some cases. After experiencing a great loss, such as the death of a loved one, make an appointment with your family physician for a physical.

• Even Jesus cried when his friend Lazarus died (John 11:35).

Even Jesus felt the loss of Lazarus when he died.

Mary   Martha

THE TOP 10 ATTRIBUTES TO LOOK FOR IN A SPOUSE

While no single personality trait can predict a compatible marriage, the following list frames the basic things to look for in a spouse. With all attributes, some differences can be the source of a couple's strength rather than a source of difficulty. Statistically, Mennonites appear to be about as successful at choosing a spouse as other people.

1 Similar values.
Values that concern religious beliefs, church service, life purpose, financial priorities, and children are a foundation on which to build the relationship. Contrary values tend to create discord.

2 Physical-energy and physical-space compatibility.
Consider whether the person's energy level and physical-space needs work with yours. Also, the word *compatibility* can mean a complementary match of opposites, or it can denote a match based on strong similarities.

3 Physical and romantic compatibility.
If the two of you have a similar degree of interest in or need for physical and romantic expression in your relationship, the chance of lifelong compatibility increases.

4 Intellectual parity.
Communicating with someone who has a significantly different intelligence level or educational background can require extra effort.

5 Emotional maturity.

A lifelong relationship of mutual challenge and support often helps each person grow emotionally, but a lifetime spent waiting for someone to grow up could be more frustration than it's worth.

6 Sense of humor.

Sense of humor can provide an excellent measure of a person's personality and an important means to couple survival. If he or she doesn't get your jokes, you could be asking for trouble.

7 Respect.

Look for someone who listens to you without trying to control you. Look also for a healthy sense of self-respect.

8 Trustworthiness.

Seek out someone who is honest and acts with your best interests in mind—not only his or hers—and tries to learn from his or her mistakes.

9 Forgiving.

When you sincerely apologize to your spouse, he or she should try to work through and get beyond the problem rather than hold on to it. Once forgiven, past mistakes should not be raised, especially in conflict situations.

10 Kindness.

An attitude of consistent kindness may be the most critical attribute for a lifelong partnership.

Be Aware

- If you live to be old, you will probably experience major changes that you cannot predict at age 15 or 25 or 35. Accepting this fact in advance can help you weather difficult times.

- Use all of your resources—intuition, emotions, and rational thought—to make the decision about a life partner.

- Family members and trusted friends can offer invaluable advice in this decision-making process and should be consulted.

- Marriage is for a lifetime and its seriousness cannot be over-stated (Mark 10:2-12). Marriage counseling with the pastor who will be performing the ceremony is a good exercise in final precautions.

HOW TO ENCOUNTER THE HOLY TRINITY AS ONE GOD IN THREE PERSONS

The Trinity is a mystery. Even great theologians don't completely understand, and some scholars spend their whole lives studying it. After 2,000 years, Christians still believe in this mystery because it gives life and shape to everything in our lives—our relationships, our faith, and especially our worship.

1 Read the sections on "God," "Jesus," and "Holy Spirit" in *Confession of Faith in a Mennonite Perspective* (Herald Press, 1995); see pages 198-202 in this book for a summary of that document.
These sections, with many biblical references to guide you, will help you to get to know the character and role of the three different entities of the Trinity.

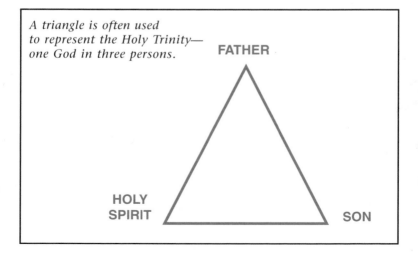

A triangle is often used to represent the Holy Trinity— one God in three persons.

FATHER

HOLY SPIRIT

SON

2 Understand that you were made in God's image.
Just as the one God is Father, Son, and Holy Spirit all at
once, you are mind, body, and soul all at once. Because you
reflect the image of God, you were made to live a life of
worship in which everything you do and say honors God.

3 Spend time in the community of faith.
Participate in worship, fellowship, Bible study, Sunday
school, service projects, and anything else that regularly
keeps you in the company of other Christians.

4 Seek out God's Word and the means of grace.
The Trinity is revealed in reading the Bible, preaching, the
sacraments, the forgiveness of sins, the community of
believers, and within anything else where Jesus, the living
Word, is active.

Be Aware

• Some people use handy metaphors to begin to get a handle
on the doctrine of the Trinity. For example, water takes three
major forms: liquid, solid, and gas. Yet it remains one substance. Such metaphors are very useful to a point, but ultimately they must give way to the divine mystery that
remains.

BIBLE STUFF

Written down by many people over hundreds of years, the Bible is more like a portable bookshelf than one book by itself. And because the Bible is God's Word, people often feel overwhelmed when they try to read it.

This section includes:

- Helpful information about when, where, and why people wrote the 66 books within the Bible. (It didn't all come together at once.)

- Tips for reading and understanding the Bible—how it's organized and what it says.

- Some of the most mystifying, hair-raising, and just plain off-the-wall stories in the Bible.

COMMON TRANSLATIONS OF THE BIBLE

Translation	Grade Level *	Theological Affiliation	Year Released	Special Features
King James Version	12.0	Church of England, conservative and evangelical	1611	Poetic style using Elizabethan English. Most widely used translation for centuries.
New American Standard Bible	11.0	Conservative and evangelical	1971; updated, 1995	Revision of the 1901 American Standard Version into contemporary language.
New Revised Standard Version	8.1	Mainline and interconfessional	1989	Updated version of the Revised Standard Version.
New King James Version	8.0	Transnational, transdenominational, conservative, and evangelical	1982	Updates the King James text into contemporary language.
New International Version	7.8	Transnational, transdenominational, conservative, and evangelical	1978; revised, 1984	Popular modern-language version. Attempts to balance literal and dynamic translation methods.
Today's New International Version	7.8	Transnational, transdenominational, conservative, and	2005	Popular modern-language version. It uses updated language to

	Grade level*	Classification	Date	Description
the Good News Bible)				
New American Bible	6.6	Roman Catholic	1970; revised NT, 1986; revised Psalms, 1991	Official translation of the Roman Catholic Church in the United States.
New Living Translation	6.4	Evangelical	1996	A meaning-for-meaning translation. Successor to the Living Bible.
New Century Version	5.6	Conservative and evangelical	1988; revised, 1991	Follows the *Living Word Vocabulary*.
Contemporary English Version	5.4	Conservative, evangelical, mainline	1995	Easy-to-read English for new Bible readers.
The Message	4.8, from NT samples	Evangelical	2002	An expressive paraphrase of the Bible.

* The grade level on which the text is written, using Dale-chall, Fry, Rygor, and Spache Formulas.

Bible classifications

Apocrypha Bible: Contains certain books that Protestants don't consider canonical. Most of these OT books are accepted by the Roman Catholic Church.

Children's Bible: Includes illustrations and other study aids that are especially helpful for children.

Concordance Bible: Lists places in the Bible where key words are found.

Red Letter Bible: The words spoken by Christ appear in red.

Reference Bible: Pages include references to other Bible passages on the same subject.

Self-Proclaiming Bible: Diacritical marks (as in a dictionary) appear above difficult names and words to help with the pronunciation.

Text Bible: Contains text without footnotes or column references. May include maps, illustrations, and other helpful material.

60 ESSENTIAL BIBLE STORIES

Story	Bible Text	Key Verse
1. Creation	Genesis 1-2	Genesis 1:27
2. The Human Condition	Genesis 3-4	Genesis 3:5
3. The Flood and the First Covenant	Genesis 6-9	Genesis 9:8
4. The Tower of Babel and Abraham and Sarah	Genesis 11-12	Genesis 12:1
5. Sarah, Hagar, and Abraham	Genesis 12-25	Genesis 17:19
6. Isaac and Rebecca	Genesis 22-25	Genesis 24:67
7. Jacob and Esau	Genesis 25-36	Genesis 28:15
8. Joseph and God's Hidden Ways	Genesis 37-50	Genesis 50:20
9. Moses and Pharaoh	Exodus 1-15	Exodus 2:23
10. The Ten Commandments	Exodus 20	Exodus 20:2
11. From the Wilderness into the Promised Land	Exodus 16-18; Deuteronomy 1-6; Joshua 1-3, 24	Deuteronomy 6:4
12. Judges	Book of Judges	Judges 21:25
13. Ruth	Book of Ruth	Ruth 4:14
14. Samuel and Saul	1 Samuel 1-11	1 Samuel 3:1
15. King David	multiple OT books	1 Samuel 8:6
16. David, Nathan, and What Is a Prophet?	2 Samuel 11-12	2 Samuel 7:12
17. Solomon	1 Kings 1-11	1 Kings 6:12
18. Split of the Kingdom	1 Kings 11ff.	1 Kings 12:16
19. Northern Kingdom, Its Prophets and Fate	1 Kings—2 Kings 17	Amos 5:21
20. Southern Kingdom, Its Prophets and Fate (Part 1)	multiple OT books	Isaiah 5:7

60 ESSENTIAL BIBLE STORIES

Story	Bible Text	Key Verse
21. Southern Kingdom, Its Prophets and Fate (Part 2)	multiple OT books	Jeremiah 31:31
22. The Exile	Isaiah 40-55; Ezekiel	Isaiah 40:10
23. Return from Exile	multiple OT books	Ezra 1:1
24. Ezra and Nehemiah	Books of Ezra and Nehemiah	Ezra 3:10
25. Esther	Book of Esther	Esther 4:14
26. Job	Book of Job	Job 1:1
27. Daniel	Book of Daniel	Daniel 3:17
28. Psalms of Praise and Trust	Psalms 8, 30, 100, 113, 121	Psalm 121:1
29. Psalms for Help	various psalms	Psalm 22:1
30. Wisdom	Job, Proverbs, Ecclesiastes	Proverbs 1:7
31. The Annunciation	Luke 1:26-56	Luke 1:31-33
32. Magi	Matthew 2:1-12	Matthew 2:2-3
33. Birth of Jesus	Luke 2:1-20	Luke 2:10-11
34. Simeon	Luke 2:25-35	Luke 2:30-32
35. Wilderness Temptations	Matthew 4:1-11; Mark 1:12-13; Luke 4:1-13	Luke 4:12-13
36. Jesus' Nazareth Sermon	Matthew 13:54-58; Mark 6:1-6; Luke 4:16-30	Luke 4:18-19, 21
37. Jesus Calls the First Disciples	Matthew 4:18-22; Mark 1:16-20; Luke 5:1-11	Luke 5:9-10
38. Beatitudes	Matthew 5:3-12	Luke 6:20-26
39. Gerasene Demoniac	Matthew 8:28-34; Mark 5:1-20; Luke 8:26-39	Luke 8:39
40. Feeding of the 5,000	Matthew 14:13-21; Mark 6:30-44; Luke 9:10-17; John 6:1-14	Luke 9:16-17

60 ESSENTIAL BIBLE STORIES

Story	Bible Text	Key Verse
41. The Transfiguration	Matthew 17:1-8; Mark 9:2-8; Luke 9:28-36	Luke 9:34-35
42. Sending of the Seventy	Matthew 8:19-22; Luke 10:1-16	Luke 10:8, 16
43. Good Samaritan	Luke 10:25-37	Luke 10:27-28
44. Healing the Bent-Over Woman	Luke 13:10-17	Luke 13:16
45. Parables of Lost and Found	Luke 15:1-32	Luke 15:31-32
46. Rich Man and Lazarus	Luke 16:19-31	Luke 16:29-31
47. Zacchaeus	Luke 19:1-11	Luke 19:9
48. Sheep and Goats	Matthew 25:31-46	Matthew 25:40
49. Parable of the Vineyard	Matthew 21:33-46; Mark 12:1-12; Luke 20:9-19; (Isaiah 5:1-7)	Luke 20:14-16
50. The Last Supper	Matthew 26:20-29; Mark 14:12-16; Luke 22:14-38	Luke 22:19-20, 27
51. Crucifixion	Matthew 27; Mark 15; Luke 23; John 19	Luke 23:42-43, 46
52. Road to Emmaus	Luke 24	Luke 24:30-31
53. Pentecost	Acts 2:1-21	Acts 2:17-18
54. Healing the Lame Man	Acts 3-4	Acts 4:19
55. Baptism of the Ethiopian	Acts 8:26-39	Acts 8:35-37
56. Call of Saul	Acts 7:58—8:1, 9:1-30	Acts 9:15-16
57. Peter and Cornelius	Acts 10	Acts 10:34-35
58. Philippians Humility	Philippians 2:1-13	Philippians 2:12-13
59. Love Hymn	1 Corinthians 13	1 Corinthians 13:4-7
60. Resurrection	1 Corinthians 15	1 Corinthians 15:51-55

HOW TO READ THE BIBLE

The Bible is a collection of 66 separate books gathered together over hundreds of years and thousands of miles. Divided into the Old Testament (Hebrew language) and the New Testament (Greek language), these writings have many authors and take many forms.

The Bible includes histories, stories, prophecies, poetry, songs, teachings, and laws, to name a few. Christians believe the Bible is the story of God's relationship with humankind and a powerful way that God speaks to people.

❶ Determine your purpose for reading.
Clarify in your own mind what you hope to gain. Your motivations should be well intentioned, such as to seek information, to gain a deeper understanding of God and yourself, or to enrich your faith. Pray for insight before every reading time.

❷ Resolve to read daily.
Commit to a daily regimen of Bible reading. Make it a part of your routine until it becomes an unbreakable habit.

Commit to read the Bible daily.

❸ Master the mechanics.
• Memorize the books of the Bible in order.

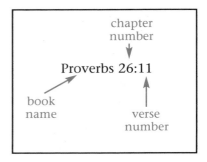

• Familiarize yourself with the introductory material. Many Bible translations include helpful information at the front of the Bible and at the beginning of each book.

• The books are broken down into chapters and verses. Locate the beginning of a book by using the Bible's table of contents. Follow the numerical chapter numbers; these are usually in large type. Verses are likewise numbered in order within each chapter. Simply run your finger down the page until you locate the verse number you're looking for.

• If your Bible contains maps (usually in the back), consult them when cities, mountains, or seas are mentioned in your reading.

❹ Befriend the written text.
Read with a pen or pencil in hand and underline passages of interest. Look up unfamiliar words in a dictionary. Write notes in the margins when necessary. The Bible was written to be read and used, not worshipped.

❺ Practice reading out loud from the Bible.

HOW TO MEMORIZE
A BIBLE VERSE

Memorizing Scripture is an ancient faith practice. Its value is often mentioned by people who have, in crisis situations, remembered comforting or reassuring passages coming to mind, sometimes decades after first memorizing them. There are three common methods of memorization.

Method 1: Memorize with Music

Choose a verse that is special for you. It is more difficult to remember something that doesn't make sense to you or that lacks meaning.

1 Choose a familiar tune.
Pick something catchy and repetitious.

2 Add the words from the Bible verse to your tune.
Mix up the words a bit, if necessary. Memorizing a verse "word for word" isn't always as important as learning the message of the verse.

3 Mark the verse in your Bible.
This will help you find it again later on. Consider highlighting or underlining it.

4 Make the words rhyme, if possible.

Method 2: The Three S's
(See it, Say it, Script it)

This method works on the principle of multisensory reinforcement. The brain creates many more neural pathways to a memory through sight, speech, and manipulation (writing) than just one of these, so recall is quicker and easier.

❶ Write the verse on index cards in large print.
Post the cards in places you regularly look, such as the refrigerator door or bathroom mirror.

❷ Say the verse out loud.
Repeat the verse 10 times to yourself every time you notice one of your index cards.

❸ Write the verse down.

❹ Try saying and writing the verse at the same time.
Repeat.

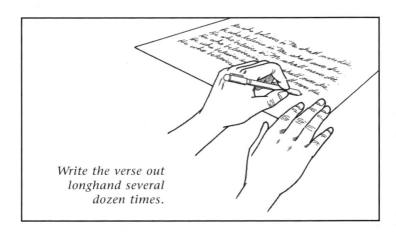

Write the verse out longhand several dozen times.

Method 3: Old-Fashioned Memorization

Attempt this method only if you consider yourself to be "old school" or if the other methods fail.

1 Write the verse out by hand on paper.
A whiteboard can work extremely well, also. Consider writing it as many as 100 times. Repeat this process until you can recite the verse flawlessly.

2 Don't get up until you've memorized the verse.
Open your Bible to the appropriate verse, sit down in front of it, and don't get up, eat, sleep, or use the bathroom until you can recite it flawlessly.

3 Enlist a family member or friend to help you.
Have them read along with you and prompt you when you get stuck.

THE TOP 10 BIBLE VILLAINS

❶ Satan

The Evil One is known by many names in the Bible and appears many places, but the devil's purpose is always the same: to disrupt and confuse people so they turn from God and seek to become their own gods. This Bible villain is still active today.

❷ The Serpent

In Eden, the serpent succeeded in tempting Eve to eat from the tree of the knowledge of good and evil (Genesis 3:1-7). As a result, sin entered creation. If it weren't for the serpent, we'd all still be walking around naked, eating fresh fruit, and living forever.

❸ Pharaoh (probably Seti I or Rameses II)

The notorious Pharaoh from the book of Exodus enslaved the Israelites. Moses eventually begged him to "Let my people go," but Pharaoh hardened his heart and refused. Ten nasty plagues later, Pharaoh relented, but then changed his mind again. In the end, with his army at the bottom of the sea, Pharaoh finally gave his slaves up to the wilderness.

❹ Goliath

"The Philistine of Gath," who stood six cubits in height (about nine feet tall), was sent to fight David, still a downy-headed youth of 15. Goliath was a fighting champion known for killing people, but David drilled Goliath in the head with a rock from his sling and gave God the glory (1 Samuel 17).

Though physically powerful, Goliath lost his battle with young David, one of the top 10 heroes of the Bible.

one cubit

Goliath   David

5 Jezebel

King Ahab of Judah's wife and a follower of the false god Baal, Jezebel led her husband away from God and tried to kill off the prophets of the Lord. Elijah the prophet, however, was on the scene. He shamed Jezebel's false prophets and killed them (1 Kings 18:40).

6 King Herod

Afraid of any potential threat to his power, Herod upon hearing about the birth of the Messiah in Bethlehem sent the Wise Men to pinpoint his location. Awestruck by the Savior in the cradle, the Wise Men went home by a different route and avoided Herod. In a rage, he ordered the murder of every child two years of age or younger in the vicinity of Bethlehem. The baby Messiah escaped with his parents to Egypt (Matthew 2:14-15).

7 The Pharisees, Sadducees, and Scribes

They dogged Jesus throughout his ministry, alternately challenging his authority and being awed by his power. It was their leadership, with the consent and blessing of the people and the Roman government that brought Jesus to trial and execution.

8 Judas

One of Jesus' original disciples, Judas earned 30 pieces of silver by betraying his Lord to the authorities. He accomplished this by leading the soldiers into the garden of Gethsemane where he revealed Jesus with a kiss (Matthew 26–27).

9 Pontius Pilate

The consummate politician, the Roman governor chose to preserve his own bloated status by giving the people what they wanted: Jesus' crucifixion. He washed his hands to signify self-absolution, but bloodied them instead.

10 God's People

They whine, they sin, they turn their backs on God over and over again. When given freedom, they blow it. When God's prophets preach repentance, God's people stone them. When offered a Savior, they kill him. In the end, it must be admitted, God's people—us!—don't really shine. Only by God's grace and the gift of faith in Jesus Christ do we have hope.

THE TOP 10 BIBLE HEROES

The Bible is filled with typical examples of heroism, but another kind of hero inhabits the pages of the Bible—those people who, against all odds, follow God no matter the outcome. These are heroes of faith.

❶ Noah

In the face of ridicule from others, Noah trusted God when God chose him to build an ark to save a remnant of humanity from destruction. Noah's trust became part of a covenant with God.

Noah trusted God, even though others made fun of him. By following God's instructions and building a great ark, Noah and his family survived the flood (Genesis 6–10).

② Abraham and Sarah

Abraham and Sarah answered God's call to leave their home and travel to a strange land, where even at advanced age they became the literal parents of God's people.

③ Moses

Moses, a man with a speech impediment, challenged the Egyptian powers to deliver God's people from bondage. He led a rebellious and contrary people for 40 years through the wilderness and gave them God's law.

④ Rahab

A prostitute who helped Israel conquer the promised land, Rahab was the great-grandmother of King David and thus a part of the family of Jesus himself.

⑤ David

Great King David, the youngest and smallest member of his family, defeated great enemies, turning Israel into a world power. He wrote psalms, led armies, and confessed his sins to the Lord.

⑥ Mary and Joseph

These humble peasants responded to God's call to be the parents of the Messiah, although the call came through a pregnancy that was not the result of marriage.

⑦ The Canaanite Woman

Desperate for her daughter's health, the Canaanite woman challenged Jesus regarding women and race by claiming God's love for all people (Matthew 15:21-28). Because of this, Jesus praised her faith.

8 Peter

Peter was a man quick to speak but slow to think. At Jesus' trial, Peter denied ever having known him. But in the power of forgiveness and through Christ's appointment, Peter became a leader in the early church.

9 Saul/Paul

Originally an enemy and persecutor of Christians, Paul experienced a powerful vision of Jesus, converted, and became the greatest missionary the church has ever known.

10 Phoebe

A contemporary of Paul's, Phoebe is believed to have delivered the book of Romans after traveling some 800 miles from Cenchrea near Corinth to Rome. A wealthy woman, she used her influence to travel, to protect other believers, and to host worship services in her home.

Phoebe is believed to have delivered the book of Romans after traveling 800 miles.

THE THREE MOST REBELLIOUS THINGS JESUS DID

1 The prophet returned to his hometown (Luke 4:14-27). Jesus returned to Nazareth, where he was raised, and was invited to read Scripture and preach. First, he insisted that the scriptures he read were not just comforting promises of a distant future, but that they were about him, a local boy, anointed by God. Second, he insisted God would bless foreigners with those same promises through him. These statements amounted to the unpardonable crime of blasphemy!

2 The rebel thumbed his nose at the authorities (John 11:55—12:11). Jesus had become an outlaw, hunted by the religious authorities who wanted to kill him. Mary, Martha, and Lazarus threw a thank-you party for Jesus in Bethany, right outside Jerusalem, the authorities' stronghold. In spite of the threats to his life, Jesus went to the party. This was not just rebellion but a demonstration of how much Jesus loved his friends.

3 The king rode a donkey in a royal procession (Matthew 21:1-17; Mark 11:1-10; Luke 19:28-38; John 12:12-19). Jesus entered Jerusalem during a great festival, before adoring crowds, as a king come to rule but not as they expected. Riding a donkey, heralded by the people with cloaks and branches, he was accompanied by the royal anthem (Psalm 118). He rode in to claim Jerusalem for God and himself as God's anointed. The Roman overlords and the Jewish leaders watched this seditious act and prepared for a crucifixion.

THE SEVEN FUNNIEST BIBLE STORIES

Humor isn't scarce in the Bible; you just have to look for it. For example, God tells Abraham (100 years old) and Sarah (in her 90s) they'll soon have a son. Understandably, they laugh. Later, they have a son named Isaac, which means "he laughs." Bible humor is also ironic, gross, and sometimes just plain bizarre.

❶ Gideon's dog-men (Judges 6:11—7:23).
God chooses Gideon to lead an army against the Midianites. Gideon gathers an army of 32,000 men, but this is too many. God tells Gideon to make all the men drink from a stream and then selects only the 300 men who lap water like dogs.

❷ David ambushes Saul in a cave while he's "busy" (1 Samuel 24:2-7).
While pursuing David cross-country to engage him in battle, Saul goes into a cave to "relieve himself" (move his bowels). Unbeknownst to Saul, David and his men are already hiding in the very same cave. While Saul's doing his business, David sneaks up and cuts off a corner of Saul's cloak with a knife. Outside afterward, David shows King Saul the piece of cloth to prove he could have killed him "on the throne."

❸ King David does the goofy (2 Samuel 12-23).
David is so excited about bringing the Ark of the Covenant to Jerusalem that he dances before God and all the people dressed only in a linen ephod, an apron-like garment that covered only the front of his body.

The doomed city of Sodom

Lot's wife ignored God's warning. She looked back at the city of Sodom and became a pillar of salt.

Pillar of salt (formerly Lot's wife)

4 Lot's wife (Genesis 19:24-26).
While fleeing God's wrath upon the cities of Sodom and Gomorrah, Lot's wife forgets (or ignores) God's warning not to look back upon the destruction and turns into a woman-sized pillar of salt.

5 Gerasene demoniac (Mark 5:1-20).
A man is possessed by so many demons that chains cannot hold him. Jesus exorcises the demons and sends them into a herd of 2,000 pigs, which then run over the edge of a cliff and drown in the sea. The herders, now 2,000 pigs poorer, get miffed and ask Jesus to leave.

6 Disciples and loaves of bread (Mark 8:14-21).
The disciples were there when Jesus fed 5,000 people with just five loaves of bread and two fish. They also saw him feed 4,000 people with seven loaves. Later, in a boat, the disciples fret to an exasperated Jesus because they have only one loaf for 13 people.

7 Peter can't swim (Matthew 14:22-33).
Blundering Peter sees Jesus walking on the water and wants to join him. But when the wind picks up, Peter panics and starts to sink. In Greek, the name Peter means "rock."

Peter, "the rock," sank when he looked to himself instead of to Jesus. Jesus later described Peter as a Rock of the church (Matthew 16:18)

THE FIVE GROSSEST BIBLE STORIES

❶ Eglon and Ehud (Judges 3:12-30).
Before kings reigned over Israel, judges ruled the people. At that time, a very overweight king named Eglon conquered Israel and demanded money. A man named Ehud brought the payment to Eglon while he was perched on his "throne" (meaning "toilet"). Along with the money, Ehud handed over a little something extra—his sword, which he buried so far in Eglon's belly that the sword disappeared into the king's fat and, as the Bible says, "the dirt came out" (v. 22).

❷ Job's sores (Job 2:1-10).
Job lived a righteous life yet he suffered anyway. He had oozing sores from the bald spot on top of his head clear down to the soft spot on the bottom of his foot. Job used a broken piece of pottery to scrape away the pus that leaked from his sores.

❸ The naked prophet (Isaiah 20).
God's prophets went to great lengths to get God's message across to the people. Isaiah was no exception. God's people planned a war, but God gave it the thumbs down. Isaiah marched around Jerusalem naked for three years as a sign of what would happen if the people went to war.

Jeremiah strapped on some filthy underwear to show God could no longer be proud of his people.

Filthy underwear

❹ **The almost-naked prophet (Jeremiah 13:1-11).**
God sent Jeremiah to announce that God could no longer be proud of the people. To make the point, Jeremiah bought a new pair of underclothes, wore them every day without washing them, then buried them in the wet river sand. Later, he dug them up, strapped them on, and shouted that this is what has happened to the people who were God's pride!

❺ **Spilling your guts (Matthew 27:1-8; Acts 1:16-19).**
Judas betrayed Jesus and sold him out for 30 pieces of silver. He bought a field with the ill-gotten loot. Guilt-stricken, Judas walked out to the field, his belly swelled up until it burst, and his intestines spilled out on to the ground.

FIVE FACTS ABOUT LIFE IN OLD TESTAMENT TIMES

1 Almost everyone wore sandals.
They were called "sandals" because people walked on sand much of the time.

2 There were no newspapers.
People got news by hearing it from other people. Spreading important news was like a giant game of "telephone."

3 It was dark.
Homes, often tents, were typically lit at night by an oil lamp, if at all.

4 You had to fetch your water, which was scarce.
Rich folks had servants to carry it for them, but most people had to carry household water in jugs or leather bags, usually some distance, from a river or well.

5 Life expectancy was short.
Despite some long-lived exceptions described in the book of Genesis, such as Abraham (175 years) and Methuselah (969 years), few people lived past 50.

Sandals were made for walking on sand.

TEN IMPORTANT THINGS THAT HAPPENED BETWEEN THE OLD AND NEW TESTAMENTS

The period of time described in the Old Testament ended about 400 years before Jesus' birth. The people of God kept living, believing, struggling, and writing during that period. Here are some of the important events that took place between the Testaments.

① The Hebrew nation dissolved.
In 587 BC, the Babylonians destroyed Jerusalem and Solomon's temple and took the people into exile. Judah was never again an independent kingdom.

② The people scattered.
After the exile to Babylon ended, the people of Judah moved to many different places. Some of them later came back, but many never did. Some of them lived in Babylon, some lived in Egypt, and some just scattered elsewhere.

③ A religion replaced a nation.
As a result of items 1 and 2, the people's religion changed. They no longer had a state or national religion (Judean religion). Instead, they had a freestanding faith called Judaism.

4 The Aramaic language became popular.
Because Aramaic was the international language of the
Persian Empire, many Jews quit speaking Hebrew and spoke
Aramaic instead. This is why Jesus spoke Aramaic.

5 Alexander the Great conquered the world.
Around 330 BC, Alexander the Great conquered the
Mediterranean and Mesopotamian world. As a result, Greek
became the everyday language of business and trade in the
region. This is why the New Testament was written in
Greek.

6 The hammer dropped.
Around 170 BC, the Seleucid emperor outlawed circumci-
sion and the Sabbath and defiled the temple. A family of
Jews called the Maccabees (which means "hammer") led a
revolt.

7 The Hebrew Scriptures were finished.
During this time, the individual books that make up what
we call the Old Testament were finished. Several other
religious books written at this time (mostly in Greek) aren't
in the Protestant Bible but are part of the Apocrypha.

8 The Sadducees, Pharisees, Essenes, Samaritans, Zealots,
and other groups of people sprouted up.
Different schools of thought developed within Judaism.
Most of their disagreements were over the idea that God's
people would be resurrected to eternal life.

9 **God seemed to have forgotten the promise.**
God promised King David that one of his descendants
would always be king in Jerusalem. But after the Babylonian
exile, there were no kings in Jerusalem. People wondered
what had happened to God's promise.

10 **The Roman Empire expanded.**
In 63 BC, the Roman Empire conquered Palestine, having
already conquered pretty much everyone else in the region.
This is why the Roman Empire ruled the area during the
time of Jesus and the New Testament.

FIVE FACTS ABOUT LIFE IN NEW TESTAMENT TIMES

1 Synagogues were not always buildings.

For worship, Jesus' people gathered in all kinds of places, often outdoors. "Church" was any gathering of people for worship.

2 Houses were boxy.

Most houses had a flat roof with an outside staircase leading to it. Inhabitants would sleep on the roof during hot weather.

Houses in New Testament times were boxy.

❸ **Every town had a marketplace.**
Usually there was just one marketplace per town, but one could buy almost everything needed to live.

❹ **People ate a lot of fish.**
The most common fish in the Sea of Galilee were catfish and carp. Roasting over a charcoal fire was the most common method of cooking.

❺ **Dogs were shunned.**
The Jewish people in Jesus' day did not keep dogs as pets. Dogs were considered unclean because they ate garbage and animal carcasses.

THE FIVE BIGGEST MISCONCEPTIONS ABOUT THE BIBLE

1 The Bible was written in a short period of time.
Christians believe that God inspired the Bible writers, the first of whom may have been Moses. God inspired people to write down important histories, traditions, songs, wise sayings, poetry, and prophetic words. All told—from the first recordings of the stories in Genesis to the last decisions about Revelation—the entire Bible was formed over a period spanning anywhere from 800 to 1,400 years.

2 One person wrote the Bible.
Unlike Islam's Qur'an, which was written by the prophet Muhammad, the books of the Bible claim the handiwork of many people. Much of Scripture does not identify the human hand that wrote it, so some parts of the Bible may have been written by women as well as men.

3 The entire Bible should be taken literally.
While many parts of the Bible are meant as descriptions of actual historical events, other parts are intended as illustrations of God's truth, such as Song of Solomon, the book of Revelation, and Jesus' parable of the Good Samaritan. So when Jesus says, "If your right eye causes you to sin, tear it out and throw it away" (Matthew 5:29), please do not take the saying literally.

❹ People in Bible times were unenlightened.
During the 1,400 years it took to write the Bible, some of history's greatest thinkers lived and worked. Many of these philosophers, architects, mathematicians, orators, theologians, historians, doctors, military tacticians, inventors, engineers, poets, and playwrights are still quoted today, and their works are still in use.

❺ The Bible is a single book.
The Bible is actually a collection of books, letters, and other writings—more like a library than a book. There are 39 books in the Hebrew scriptures, what Christians call the "Old" Testament, and 27 books (mostly letters) in the New Testament. There are seven books in the Apocryhpha (books written between the Old and New Testaments), or "deuterocanonical" books.

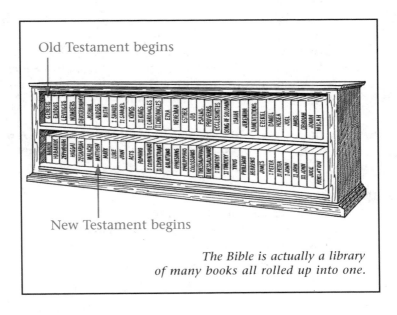

Old Testament begins

New Testament begins

The Bible is actually a library of many books all rolled up into one.

JESUS' TWELVE APOSTLES (PLUS JUDAS AND PAUL)

While Jesus had many disciples (students and followers) the Bible focuses particularly on twelve who were closest to him. Tradition says that these twelve spread Jesus' message throughout the known world (Matthew 28:18-20). For this reason, they were known as apostles, a word that means "sent ones."

❶ Andrew
A fisherman and the first disciple to follow Jesus, Andrew brought his brother, Simon Peter, to Jesus.

❷ Bartholomew
Also called Nathanael, tradition has it that he was martyred by being skinned alive.

❸ James the Elder
James, with John and Peter, was one of Jesus' closest disciples. Herod Agrippa killed James because of his faith, which made him a martyr (Acts 12:2).

❹ John
John (or one of his followers) is thought to be the author of the Gospel of John and three letters of John. He probably died of natural causes in old age.

❺ Matthew
Matthew was a tax collector and therefore probably an outcast even among his own people. The Gospel of Matthew is attributed to him.

❻ Peter

Peter was a fisherman who was brought to faith by his brother Andrew. He was probably martyred in Rome by being crucified upside down.

❼ Philip

Philip, possibly a Greek, is responsible for bringing Bartholomew (Nathanael) to faith. He is thought to have died in a city called Phrygia.

❽ James the Less

James was called "the Less" so he wouldn't be confused with James, the brother of John, or James, Jesus' brother.

❾ Simon

Simon is often called "the Zealot." Zealots were a political group in Jesus' day that favored the overthrow of the Roman government by force.

❿ Jude

Jude may have worked with Simon the Zealot in Persia (Iran) where they were martyred on the same day.

⓫ Thomas

"Doubting" Thomas preached the message of Jesus in India.

⓬ Matthias

Matthias was chosen by lot to replace Judas. It is thought that he worked mostly in Ethiopia.

⓭ Judas Iscariot

Judas was the treasurer for Jesus' disciples and the one who betrayed Jesus for 30 pieces of silver. According to the Bible, Judas killed himself for his betrayal.

⓮ Paul

Paul is considered primarily responsible for bringing non-Jewish people to faith in Jesus. He traveled extensively and wrote many letters to believers. Many of Paul's letters are included in the New Testament.

THE FIVE WEIRDEST LAWS IN THE OLD TESTAMENT

The Old Testament has many helpful, common sense laws, such as "You shall not kill" and "You shall not steal." But there are a few others that need some explaining.

1 **The "ox" law.**

"When an ox gores a man or a woman to death, the ox shall be stoned, and its flesh shall not be eaten; but the owner of the ox shall not be liable" (Exodus 21:28). Replace "ox" with "car" and the law makes more sense—it is about protecting others from reckless actions.

People living in biblical times were sometimes gored by oxen.

People who were gored by oxen—or victims of other crimes—had legal recourse.

❷ The "no kid boiling" law.

"You shall not boil a kid in its mother's milk" (Exodus 23:19b). A "kid," of course, is a juvenile goat, not a human being.

❸ The "which bugs are legal to eat" law.

"All winged insects that walk upon all fours are detestable to you. But among the winged insects that walk on all fours you may eat those that have jointed legs above their feet" (Leviticus 11:20-21). The law is unclear whether it is legal to eat the bug if you first pull off the legs.

❹ The "don't eat blood" law.

"No person among you shall eat blood" (Leviticus 17:12). Some laws beg the question whether people in that time had any sense of taste.

❺ The "pure cloth" law.

"You shall not wear clothes made of wool and linen woven together" (Deuteronomy 22:11). Polyester came along after Bible times.

THE TOP 10 BIBLE MIRACLES AND WHAT THEY MEAN

❶ Creation.
God created the universe and everything that is in it, and God continues to create and recreate without ceasing. God's first and ongoing miracle was to reveal that the creation has a purpose.

❷ The Passover.
The Israelites were enslaved by Pharaoh, a ruler who believed the people belonged to him, not to God. In the last of 10 plagues, God visited the houses of all the Egyptians to kill the firstborn male in each one. God alone is Lord of the people, and no human can claim ultimate power over us.

❸ The Exodus.
God's people were fleeing Egypt when Pharaoh dispatched his army to force them back into slavery. The army trapped the people with their backs to a sea, but God parted the water and the people walked across to freedom while Pharaoh's minions were destroyed. God chose to free us from all forms of tyranny so we may use that freedom to serve God and each other.

❹ Manna.
After the people crossed the sea to freedom, they complained that they were going to starve to death. They even asked to go back to Egypt. God sent manna, a form of bread, so the people lived. God cares for us even when we give up, pine for our slavery, and lose faith. God never abandons us.

5 The Incarnation.

The immortal and infinite God became a human being, choosing to be born of a woman. God loved us enough to become one of us in Jesus of Nazareth, forever bridging the divide that had separated us from God.

6 Jesus healed the paralyzed man.

Some men brought a paralyzed friend to Jesus. Jesus said, "Son, your sins are forgiven" (Mark 2:5). This means that Jesus has the power to forgive our sins—and he does so as a free gift.

7 Jesus calmed the storm.

Jesus was asleep in a boat with his disciples when a great storm came up and threatened to sink it. He said, "Peace! Be still!" (Mark 4:39). The storm immediately calmed. Jesus is Lord over even the powers of nature.

8 The Resurrection.

Human beings executed Jesus, but God raised him from the dead on the third day. Through baptism, we share in Jesus' death, so we will also share in eternal life with God the Father, Son, and Holy Spirit. Christ conquered death.

9 Pentecost.

Jesus ascended from the earth, but he did not leave the church powerless or alone. On the 50th day after the Jewish Passover (Pentecost means 50th); Jesus sent the Holy Spirit to create the church and take up residence among us. The Holy Spirit is present with us always.

10 The Second Coming.

One day, Christ will come again and end all suffering. This means that the final result of the epic battle between good and evil is already assured. It is simply that evil has not yet admitted defeat.

THE EXODUS

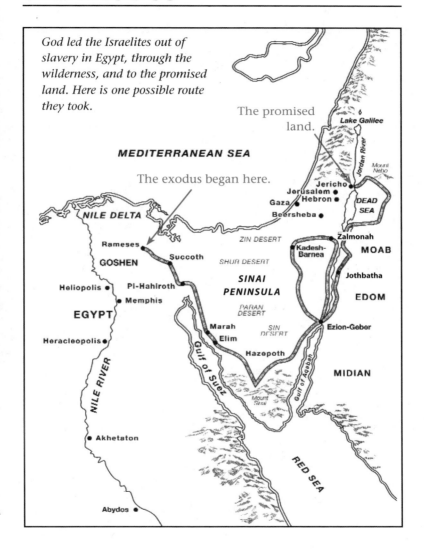

God led the Israelites out of slavery in Egypt, through the wilderness, and to the promised land. Here is one possible route they took.

The promised land.

The exodus began here.

MEDITERRANEAN SEA

Lake Galilee

Jordan River

Mount Nebo

Jericho

Jerusalem

Hebron

Gaza

DEAD SEA

Beersheba

Zalmonah

ZIN DESERT

Kadesh-Barnea

MOAB

NILE DELTA

Rameses

Succoth

SHUR DESERT

SINAI PENINSULA

Jothbatha

GOSHEN

Pi-Hahiroth

EDOM

Heliopolis

Memphis

PARAN DESERT

EGYPT

Marah

SIN DESERT

Ezion-Geber

Heracleopolis

Elim

Gulf of Suez

Hazepoth

MIDIAN

Gulf of Aqabah

NILE RIVER

Mount Sinai

Akhetaton

RED SEA

Abydos

THE HOLY LAND—
OLD TESTAMENT TIMES

The Mennonite Handbook

THE HOLY LAND—
NEW TESTAMENT TIMES

PAUL'S JOURNEYS

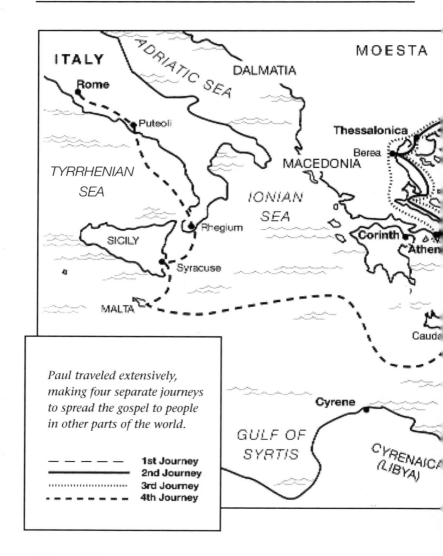

ITALY

ADRIATIC SEA

MOESTA

DALMATIA

Rome

Puteoli

TYRRHENIAN
SEA

Thessalonica

Berea

MACEDONIA

IONIAN
SEA

Rhegium

SICILY

Corinth

Athen

Syracuse

MALTA

Cauda

Paul traveled extensively,
making four separate journeys
to spread the gospel to people
in other parts of the world.

Cyrene

GULF OF
SYRTIS

CYRENAICA
(LIBYA)

– – – – –	1st Journey
————	2nd Journey
··············	3rd Journey
– ·– ·– ·–	4th Journey

JERUSALEM IN JESUS' TIME

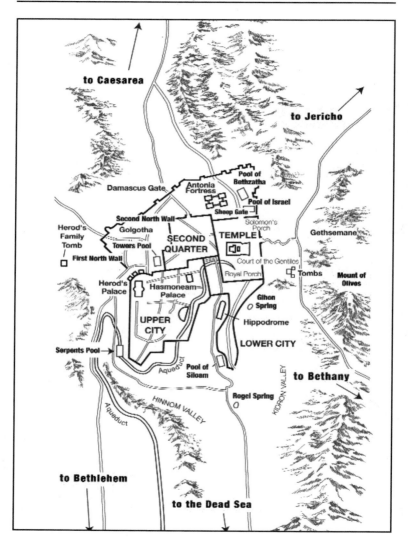

to Caesarea

to Jericho

Pool of Bethzatha

Damascus Gate

Antonia Fortress

Pool of Israel

Sheep Gate

Second North Wall

Solomon's Porch

Herod's Family Tomb

Golgotha

SECOND QUARTER

TEMPLE

Gethsemane

Towers Pool

First North Wall

Court of the Gentiles

Herod's Palace

Royal Porch

Tombs

Mount of Olives

Hasmoneam Palace

Gihon Spring

UPPER CITY

Hippodrome

LOWER CITY

Serpents Pool

Aqueduct

Pool of Siloam

Rogel Spring

HINNOM VALLEY

KIDRON VALLEY

to Bethany

Aqueduct

to Bethlehem

to the Dead Sea

NOAH'S ARK

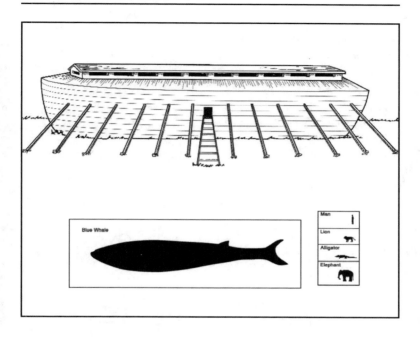

A cubit is equal to the length of a man's forearm from the elbow to the tip of the middle finger—approximately 18 inches or 45.7 centimeters. Noah's ark was 300 cubits long, 50 cubits wide, and 30 cubits tall (Genesis 6:15).

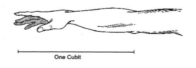

One Cubit

THE ARK OF THE COVENANT

God told the Israelites to place the stone tablets—the "covenant"—of the law into the Ark of the Covenant. The Israelites believed that God was invisibly enthroned above the vessel and went before them wherever they traveled.

*The Ark of the Covenant was
2.5 cubits long and 1.5 cubits wide
(Exodus 25:17).*

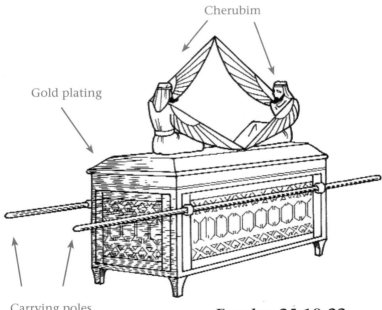

Cherubim

Gold plating

Carrying poles

Exodus 25:10-22

SOLOMON'S TEMPLE

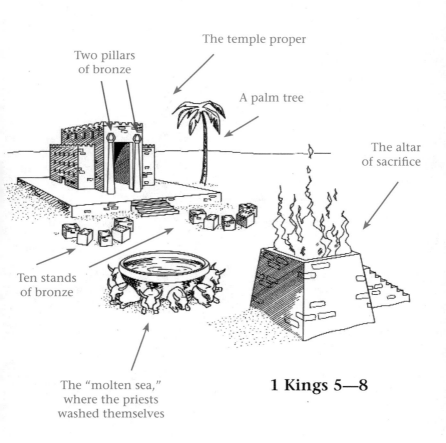

Two pillars
of bronze

The temple proper

A palm tree

The altar
of sacrifice

Ten stands
of bronze

The "molten sea,"
where the priests
washed themselves

1 Kings 5—8

THE ARMOR OF GOD

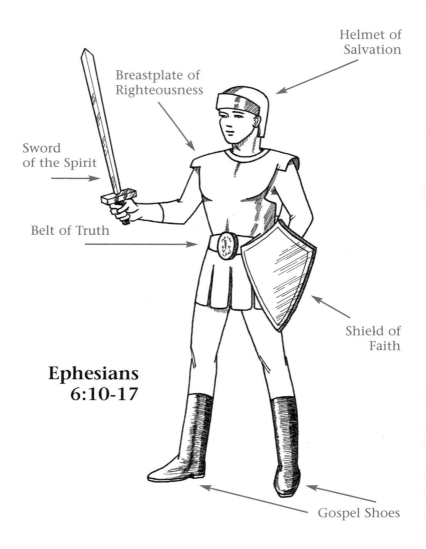

Helmet of Salvation

Breastplate of Righteousness

Sword of the Spirit

Belt of Truth

Shield of Faith

Ephesians 6:10-17

Gospel Shoes

THE PASSION AND CRUCIFIXION

Judas betrayed Jesus with a kiss, saying, "the one I will kiss is the man; arrest him" (Matthew 26:48).

Peter denied Jesus three times (Matthew 26:69-75).

Crucifixion was so common in Jesus' time that the Romans had special names for the parts of the cross.

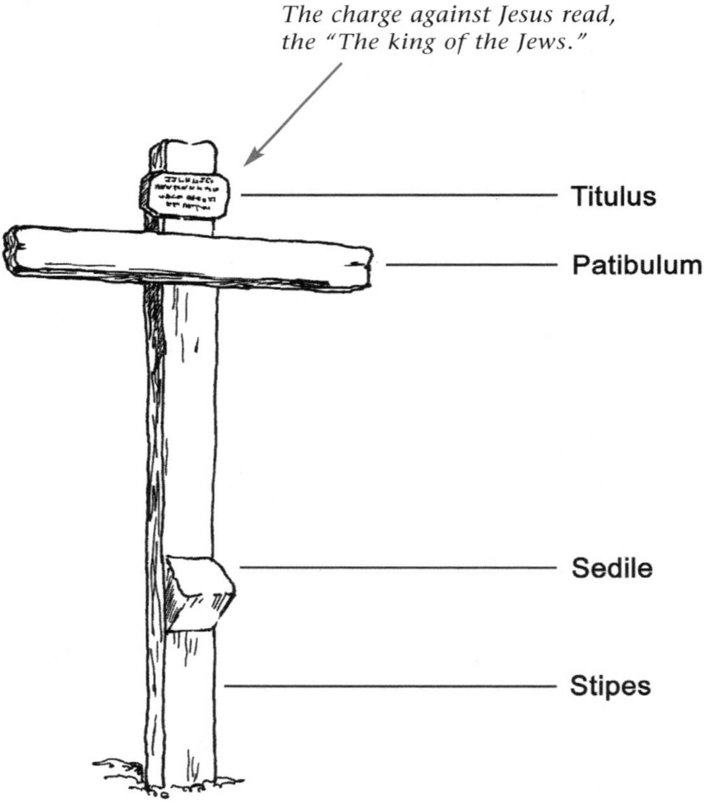

The charge against Jesus read, the "The king of the Jews."

Titulus

Patibulum

Sedile

Stipes

Eventually, the victim would be unable to lift himself to take a breath, and he would suffocate.

While the Romans broke the legs of the men who were crucified next to Jesus, they found that Jesus had already died. To make sure, they pierced his side with a spear, probably to puncture his heart (John 19:34).

Joseph of Arimathea and several women took Jesus down and carried him to the tomb (Matthew 27:57-61).

The miracle of resurrection took place three days later, when Jesus rose from the dead.

MENNONITE STUFF

Statements of what Mennonites believe have been among us from earliest beginnings. In this section you will find excerpts from these various sources. All are important, and there are many more out there for you to discover. Keep them handy for pondering during traffic jams, doctors' waiting rooms, and late night insomnia. And most importantly, when the opportunities present themselves, share them with others.

May these readings of faith encourage us to hold fast to the confession of our hope without wavering, for the One who has promised is faithful (Hebrews 10:23).

This section includes:

• A user-friendly summary of the Schleitheim Confession.

• The riveting and timeless story of Dirk Willems.

• Prayers for your day.

THE BEATITUDES

Matthew 5:3-10 KJV
(Palestinian, first century)

Blessed are the poor in spirit:
> for theirs is the kingdom of heaven.

Blessed are they who mourn:
> for they shall be comforted.

Blessed are the meek:
> for they shall inherit the earth.

Blessed are they who hunger and thirst after righteousness:
> for they shall be filled.

Blessed are the merciful:
> for they shall obtain mercy.

Blessed are the pure in heart: for they shall see God.

Blessed are the peacemakers:
> for they shall be called the children of God.

Blessed are they who are persecuted for righteousness' sake:
> for theirs is the kingdom of heaven.

Blessed are you, when men shall revile you, and persecute
> you, and shall say all manner of evil against you
> falsely for my sake. Rejoice, and be exceeding glad:
> for great is your reward in heaven: for so they persecuted
> the prophets who were before you.

THE LORD'S PRAYER

Matthew 6:9-13 KJV
(Palestinian, first century)

Our Father which art in heaven,
Hallowed be thy name.
Thy kingdom come.
Thy will be done on earth, as it is in heaven.
Give us this day our daily bread.
And forgive us our debts, as we forgive our debtors.
And lead us not into temptation, but deliver us from evil:
For thine is the kingdom, and the power, and the glory, for ever.
Amen.

THE SEVEN ARTICLES OF THE SCHLEITHEIM CONFESSION OF FAITH

A contemporary abridgement by Brinton Rutherford
(Swiss, 1527)

The articles on which we agreed at Schleitheim in Canton Schaffhausen, Switzerland, on Saint Matthias' Day, 1527 are these:

First, only those who truly repent and who confess that Christ has taken away their sins and who personally request it and who demonstrate a transformed life to the church shall be given baptism. This excludes all infant baptism.

Second, the brothers and sisters of the church shall admonish twice in secret and the third time openly those in the church who slip sometimes and fall into error and sin following the pattern of Matthew 18. This shall be done according to the regulation of the Spirit in Matthew 5 before the Lord's Supper, so that we may break and eat the bread and drink the cup in love and unity.

Third, the Lord's Supper is celebrated by those who are joined to the church in voluntary believers baptism and who are living in unity with the brothers and sisters of the church. The supper is a memorial meal and nothing more.

Fourth, the brothers and sisters of the church should live in a manner that demonstrates the clear separation between the kingdoms of this world and the kingdom of God and his Christ, the kingdom of darkness and the kingdom of light. Such a separation means that the Christian cannot participate in wielding weapons of force or the power of the state against one's enemies. As Christ said, love your enemies, and do not resist the evil person.

Fifth, the pastor in the church of God shall, as Paul said, be one who has a good reputation among non-Christians. This office shall be to read, to admonish and teach, to warn, to discipline, to ban in the church, to lead out in prayer for the growth of all the brothers and sisters, to offer the bread for the Lord's Supper, and to see to the care of the body of Christ, so that it may be built up and the one who slanders be stopped. The church shall support the needs of the pastor that they have chosen so that the one who serves the Gospel may get a living from the Gospel as the Lord has ordained. But if two or three witnesses testify to the sins of a pastor, the pastor shall be disciplined before all in order that the others may fear God. If the pastor is banished or martyred another shall be selected immediately so that the people of God may not be destroyed.

Sixth, God has ordained the use of the power of the state to punish and put to death the wicked, but the people of God are to have no part in such activity. God ordained the proper use of the power of the state to guard and protect the good. For those who follow Christ as disciples, however, only the command to sin no more, the ban, and excommunication, may be used to warn the one who has fallen into error and sinned. A Christian is forbidden to take the life of another. A Christian, who follows the example and teaching of Christ, may not employ the power of the state against the wicked for the defense and protection of the good. Neither should the Christians seek judgments against one another in a court of law. Nor should a Christian take a position with the government that wields the power of the state. Jesus walked away from that offer, and we are to follow his example.

Seventh, the use of the oath to settle an argument or to seal a promise is prohibited by Christ. We are simply to keep our word in all matters. Some do not give credence to the simple command of Christ and argue that God swore to keep his promises to Abraham; so why should not the Christian also swear when a promise is made to someone? We answer, God is unable to not keep his promises whether or not God swears, but swearing does not make people more able to keep their promises so, as Christ said, we should not swear at all. Instead we should simply let our yes mean yes and our no mean no.

DIRK WILLEMS

From the *Martyrs Mirror*, in condensed form
(Dutch, 1569)

In the year 1569 a devout, faithful brother and follower of Jesus Christ, named Dirk Willems, was apprehended at Asperen, Holland. Since his faith was founded on the firm foundation stone, Jesus Christ, rather than on the drifting sand of human commandments, Willems, standing firm against all evil winds of human doctrine and the heavy showers of tyrannical and severe persecution, remained immovable and steadfast to the very end.

Concerning Willem's arrest, it is stated by trustworthy persons, that when he fled he was hotly pursued by a thief-catcher. Since there had been some freezing weather, Willems ran across ice to escape his pursuer. He got across the ice with considerable peril but safely. The thief-catcher following him, however, broke through the ice and fell into the freezing water. When Willems realized that his adversary was in danger of losing his life, he quickly returned and helped him get out of the freezing water. By doing so, he certainly saved the thief-catcher's life.

The thief-catcher wanted to let Willems go, but the magistrate very sternly called the thief-catcher to consider his oath of service, and thus Willems was again seized by the thief-catcher. After time of harsh imprisonment accompanied by great trials coming from the deceitful followers of the Pope, Willens was executed by burning with a slow fire at Asperen by these bloodthirsty, ravening wolves. He endured it with great steadfastness and confirmed the genuine faith of the truth with his death and blood.

Concerning Willem's execution, it is related as true from the trustworthy memoirs of those who were present at the death of this devout witness of Jesus Christ that the place

Dirk Williams saves the thief-catcher by Jan Luyken

where this execution occurred was outside the town of Asperen on the side of Leerdam. Because a strong east wind was blowing that day, the bonfire was driven away from the upper part of his body as he stood tied to the stake. As a result, this good man suffered a slow, painful death, so much so, that in the town of Leerdam, toward which the wind was blowing, he was heard to exclaim over seventy times, "O my Lord; my God," and similar things. For this reason, the judge or bailiff who was present on horseback, filled with sorrow and regret at the man's sufferings, wheeled about his horse, turned his back toward the place of execution, and said to the executioner, "Dispatch the man with a quick death." But how or in what manner the executioner then dealt with this devout witness of Jesus, I have not been able to learn, except only, that his life was consumed by the fire, and that he passed through the conflict with great determination, having commended his soul into the hands of God.

SHORTER CATECHISM

From *Conversation on Saving Faith for the Young in Questions and Answers*
Gerhard Roosen
(North German, eighteenth century)

1 What compels you to join the followers of Christ and be baptized?
I am impelled by faith to separate myself from the world and its sinful lusts and to submit in obedience to my Lord, Redeemer, and Savior, for the salvation of my soul. Hebrews 5:9.

2 What compels you to take this course of action?
The will and good pleasure of God, which were proclaimed and demonstrated to me through the preaching of the Gospel, compels me. This preaching revealed to me the laws and commands of Christ, which I am bound to receive and observe in true faith. Matthew 7:21, 19:17.

3 Are you justified and saved through good works and keeping the commands of Christ?
No. Through good works alone I cannot merit salvation, for salvation is the unmerited grace of God purchased for us by Jesus Christ. Ephesians 2:8.

4 What is the purpose of doing good works and keeping the commands of Christ?
Good works are evidence of true faith in Jesus Christ. Obedience to Christ's commands out of love to God is the light and life of faith without which "faith is dead." James 2:20.

5 How is a person justified before God?
Jesus Christ alone justifies. By his righteousness we become partakers through "faith which works by love." Galatians 5:6.

6 What is true faith?

It is a certainty that what is revealed to us in Scripture is true. By faith we have full confidence that Jesus Christ has pardoned our sins, provided us his righteousness, and given us eternal life. Ephesians 2:5.

7 What do you believe?

I believe in God the Father, Son, and Holy Spirit.

8 What do you believe and confess about God the Father?

I believe with the heart and confess with the mouth that he is one, eternal, almighty, and just God, the creator and sustainer of heaven and earth, together with all things visible and invisible. Romans 10:10, Genesis 14:17.

9 What do you believe and confess about the Son?

I believe that He is Jesus Christ, Son of the living God, our savior and redeemer, who has been with the Father from eternity, and who, at "the fullness of time" was sent into the world; that He was conceived by the Holy Spirit, born of the blessed virgin Mary; suffered for us under Pontius Pilate, was crucified, died, buried, and rose again from the dead, on the third day, ascended into heaven and now sits at the right hand of God, the almighty Father, whence He will come again to judge the living and the dead. Matthew 25:31, John 17:5, Galatians 4:4.

10 What do you believe and confess about the Holy Spirit?

I believe and confess that the Holy Spirit proceeds from the Father and the Son and is divine in nature. Therefore, I also believe in God the Father, Son, and Holy Spirit as being one true God. I also confess a general, holy Christian church, the communion of saints, the remission of sins, and the resurrection of the body, followed by eternal life. 1 John 5:20, John 5:29.

11 What do you believe and confess about the holy Christian church?

I believe and confess by my faith that there is a Church of God, which the Lord Jesus purchased with His own blood, and which He sanctified and cleansed with the washing of water by the Word, that He might present it to Himself a glorious church. Ephesians 5:26, 27.

12 Of what does the church of God consist?

The church of God consists of persons who gather, through faith in Jesus Christ, and withdraw from a sinful world and submit in obedience to the Gospel. They are unwilling to live for themselves, but instead live for Christ, in true humility. They apply themselves to exercise Christian virtues by observing God's holy ordinances. Such are members of the body of Christ and heirs of eternal life. 2 Peter 1:11.

13 How and through what means is the church of God upheld?

The church is upheld through the preaching of the holy Gospel and the instruction of the Holy Ghost. Teachers and ministers are elected by the church for the purpose of carrying on and maintaining the work of God. Ephesians 4:11.

14 By what authority and how does the church choose leaders?

Just as the first apostles appointed teachers and ministers, so now God also has given power to His church to elect teachers and ministers. The appointment of ministers must take place according to the example that the apostles observed in such matters. Ephesians 4:12; Acts 1:15-26.

15 Where does the ordinance of caring for the poor come from?

We have an example of caring for the poor in the Acts of the Apostles, where the apostles, when the "number of the disciples was multiplied," called together the multitude who selected "from among them, seven men," who took charge of the necessary "business." We still observe this practice where that which is contributed by Christian hearts is given to provide for the necessities of the poor members of the church. Acts 6:1; Ephesians 4:28.

⑯ How and through what means are members of the body incorporated into the church of God?
Members of the body are joined to the church through the ordinance of Christian baptism on confession of their faith and repentance of their past sins. Upon this confession, they are baptized in the name of the Father, the Son, and the Holy Ghost. Matthew 28:19.

⑰ What is baptism?
Baptism is an external ordinance of Christ, a sign of a spiritual birth from God, a "putting on of Christ," and an incorporation into His church, an evidence that we have established a covenant with Christ. Romans 6:4; Galatians 3:27; 1 Peter 3:21.

⑱ What purpose does baptism serve?
Baptism signifies to true believers the washing away of the impurity of their souls through the blood of Christ, namely, the forgiveness of their sins, at which point they console themselves with the hope of eternal salvation through Jesus Christ, whom they have "put on" in baptism. Galatians 3:27.

⑲ To what are the members of the church of Christ bound by baptism?
Baptism binds members to the act of repenting of their past sins and being buried into Christ's death by baptism, and of binding themselves to Christ in a new life and conversation —a life of obedience—in order that they may follow His will and do what He has commanded them to do. Matthew 28:20.

20 What is the Lord's Supper?
The Supper is an external ceremony and institution of Christ, and ministered to believers in the form of bread and wine. Participating in the Supper is an act of remembrance of the death and sufferings of Christ to be declared and observed in His memory. 1 Corinthians 11:26.

21 What purpose does Lord's Supper serve?
The supper signifies for us how Christ's holy body was sacrificed on the cross, and that the precious blood Christ shed for us cleanses us of all sins. 1 John 1:7.

22 What use is the observance of the Lord's Supper to the Christian?
By the Supper, we bear witness to my simple obedience to Christ, our Savior and Redeemer. Through faith, obedience has the promise of eternal salvation, secures for us the communion of the body and blood of Christ, and comforts us with the benefit of His death, that is, the assurance of the forgiveness of our sins. 1 Corinthians 10:16; Hebrews 5:9.

23 Is marriage an institution of God?
Yes. Marriage is instituted by God Himself and confirmed in the case of Adam and Eve in the Garden of Eden. Genesis 1:27, 28.

24 Why was marriage instituted by God?
Marriage was instituted for the purpose of procreation so that the population of the earth would increase and so that the enjoyment of sexual union outside of wedlock may be avoided. Therefore "every man" is to "have his own wife," and "every woman her own husband."
1 Corinthians 7:2.

25 What should be considered before one enters into marriage?

Persons who are not too nearly related by consanguinity, may, after diligent prayer to God, enter into marriage and endeavor to live as husband and wife in a Christian manner as long as both shall live provided that they, as members of the Christian church, enter into marriage only with members of the church. Leviticus 18:6-17; 1 Corinthians 7:39; 9:5.

26 Should a member of the church marry someone with whom he or she does not agree on matters of faith and doctrine?

No. This is contrary to the marriage institution. The one who enters into matrimony without agreement on faith and doctrine acts contrary to the law of God and the doctrine of the apostles. Deuteronomy 7:3, 4; Judges 3:6, 7; 1 Corinthians 1:10; 7:39; Philippians 2:1, 2.

27 May a lawful marriage ever end in divorce?

No. Husband and wife united by the covenant of marriage are so closely bound to each other that they may never separate, except in case of fornication. Matthew 19:9.

28 What do you believe and confess about the authority of civil government?

I confess, from the testimony of Holy Scripture, that kings and governments are instituted by God for the welfare and common interest of the countries over which they rule. The one who resists such authorities, "resists the ordinance of God." Romans 13:1. Therefore, we are under obligation to fear and honor government, and obey the same in all things that do not militate against the Word of God. We are also commanded to pray for presidents and governments. 1 Timothy 1:2.

29 May a member of the church swear an oath?
No. For although taking an oath was allowed to the fathers of the Old Testament, yet has our Lord and institutor of the New Testament, Christ Jesus, expressly forbid it. Matthew 5:33-37. This is confirmed by the Apostle James, when he says: "Above all things, my brethren, swear not . . . but let your yea be yea; and your nay, nay; lest ye fall into condemnation." James 5:12.

30 May a member of the church take revenge?
No. Although the Old Testament dispensation provided the liberty to do seek revenge, now that it is totally forbidden by Christ and His apostles. We must not desire revenge, but, in meekness, do good to our neighbor and also to our enemies. Matthew 5:38, 39; Romans 12:19-21.

31 If a member of the church sins, how should the church respond?
I confess by virtue of the doctrine of Christ and His apostles that reproof and discipline must be fostered and maintained among believers. The stubborn and those who have committed gross sins and works of the flesh separate themselves from God and must be separated from the communion of believers. In this way, for their own correction, they are rebuked before all so "that others also may fear." Matthew 18:15-18; Isaiah 59:2; 1 Timothy 5:20.

32 What should be our conduct toward those who have been separated from the church?
According to the doctrine of the apostles, the true members of the church of Christ withdraw from members who have been reproved and remain impenitent offenders. We are to have no spiritual communion with them, except by chance or occasion, when they may be exhorted in love, compassion, and Christian discretion to rise from their fallen state and return to the church. Romans 16:17; Titus 3:10.

33 How long should this withdrawal from the offender be observed?

Until they return again, give evidence of repentance and sorrow for their sins, and earnestly desire again to be admitted into the communion of the church. In such case they are, after solemn prayer to God, again to be received and admitted. 2 Corinthians 2:6, 7.

34 What do you believe and confess about the second coming of Christ and the resurrection of the dead?

I believe that Christ, our Head, Lord and Savior, will just as He visibly ascended to heaven, again appear from heaven in great power and glory, "with a shout. . . and with the trumpet of God." 1 Thessalonians 4:16. "For the hour is coming, in the which all that are in the graves shall hear his voice, and shall come forth; they that have done good, unto the resurrection of life; and they that have done evil, Unto the resurrection of damnation." John 5:28, 29. "For we must all appear before the judgment seat of Christ; that every one may receive the things done in his body, according to that he hath done, whether it be good or bad." 2 Corinthians 5:10.

Now as this confession agrees with the doctrine of Christ and His apostles, we ask you, "Are you inclined with your whole heart, to submit yourself to the will of your Redeemer and Savior, Jesus Christ, to deny yourself together with all sinful lusts, and to strive by the grace of God, in true faith and heartfelt humility, to lead a pious and godly life and holy conversation, according to the commandments of God, as long as you live?

Yes.

God's grace and rich blessings are heartily wished to you through the power of the Holy Spirit, to salvation, to whom be honor and praise for ever and ever. Amen.

A SHORT AND SINCERE DECLARATION

from *Pennsylvania Mennonite Heritage*, January 1996
(Pennsylvania, 1775)

To Our Honorable Assembly, and All Others in High or Low
Station of Administration, and to All Friends and Inhabitants
of this Country to whose Sight this May Come, Be They
English or Germans
Benjamin Hershey, et al.

In the first place we acknowledge us indebted to the
most high God who created heaven and earth, the only good
being, to thank him for all his great goodness and manifold
mercies and love through our Savior Jesus Christ who is come to
save the souls of men, having all power in heaven and on earth.

Further we find ourselves indebted to be thankful to
our late worthy Assembly for their giving so good an advice
in these troublesome times to all ranks of people in
Pennsylvania, particularly in allowing those, who by the
doctrine of our Savior Jesus Christ are persuaded in their
consciences to love their enemies and not to resist Evil, to
enjoy the liberty of their conscience. Also for all the good
things we have enjoyed, we heartily thank that worthy body of
Assembly and all high and low in office who have advised to
such a peaceful measure. We are hoping and confiding that the
Assembly and all others entrusted with power in this hitherto
blessed province may be moved by the same spirit of grace
which animated the first founder of this province, our late
worthy Proprietor, William Penn, to grant liberty of conscience
to all its inhabitants;

May our rulers in the great and memorable Day of
Judgment be put on the right hand of the just Judge, who
judges without respect of person, and hear of Him these

blessed words, "Come, ye blessed of my Father, inherit the kingdom prepared for you," etc.; "What ye have done unto one of the least of these my brethren, you have done unto me," among which we by His grace hope to be ranked and numbered (i.e., the least of Christ's brethren and sisters). We hope every lenity and favor shown to such tender-conscienced, although weak followers of this our blessed Savior, will not be forgotten by Him in that great day.

The advice to those who do not find freedom of conscience to take up arms, that they ought to be helpful to those who are in need and distressed circumstances, we receive with cheerfulness towards all people of what station they may be—it being our principle to feed the hungry and give the thirsty drink. We have dedicated ourselves to serve all people in every thing that can be helpful to the preservation of other's lives, but we find no freedom in giving, or doing, or assisting in any thing by which person's lives are destroyed or hurt. We beg the patience of all those who believe we err in this point.

We are always ready, according to Christ's command to Peter, to pay the tribute, that we may offend no one; and so we are willing to pay taxes, "and to render unto Caesar those things that are Caesar's, and to God those things that are God's," although we think ourselves very weak to give God his due honor, He, being a Spirit and Life, and we, only dust and ashes.

We are also willing to be subject to the higher powers, and to give in the manner Paul directs us: "For he bears the Sword not in vain, for he is the minister of God, a avenger to execute wrath upon him that doeth evil."

This testimony we lay down before our worthy Assembly and all other persons in government, letting them know that we are thankful, as above mentioned, and that we are not at liberty in conscience to take up arms to conquer our enemies, but rather to pray to God, who has power in heaven and on earth, for us and them.

We also crave the patience of all the inhabitants of this country. What they think to see clearer in the doctrine of the blessed Jesus Christ we will leave to them and God, finding ourselves very poor. For faith is to proceed out of the Word of God, which is Life and spirit, and a Power of God, and our conscience is to be instructed by the same; therefore we beg for patience.

Our small gift, which we have given, we gave to those who have power over us that we may not offend them, as Christ taught us by the tribute penny.

We heartily pray that God would govern all hearts of our rulers, be they high or low, to meditate on those good things that will pertain to our and their happiness.

The above declaration [written by Benjamin Hershey, minister of the Menonist Church] signed by a number of elders and teachers of the Society of Menonists and some of the German Baptists, presented to the Honorable House of Assembly on the 7th day of November 1775, was most graciously received.

MORNING PRAYER

from Christian Burkholder's *Address to Youth*
(Lancaster, Pennsylvania, 1804)

Merciful God and Father, you have again permitted the sun of nature to rise "on the evil and the good." Praise and thanks to you, O gracious God for your fatherly grace and for the protection and blessings that I have enjoyed during this night. Permit me also to enjoy your blessing during this day and enlighten my dark heart with the light of your grace so that I may fully learn to understand and know my own frailties and faults.

Take me this day under the protection of your grace; fill my heart with your divine love and with true humility and self-abasement. Strengthen my faith and cause me to grow in everything that is good from day to day. Impress also deeply on my mind my perishable and transient state, so that I may be constantly on my guard. Set your Holy Spirit as a watchman over my heart, mind, and thoughts so that if this day should be my last in this world of trouble I may be found watching and so be prepared to enter into rest.

So I commend myself into your hands with body and soul and everything that I have so that nothing may be mine anymore but everything yours. In trouble and necessity grant me patience; in temptation, firmness and strength; and in prosperous and healthy days, a thankful heart. Lastly, preserve me from evil in time and in eternity, through Jesus Christ. Amen.

EVENING PRAYER

from *Prayer Book for Earnest Christians*
(Berlin, Upper Canada, 1846)

Praise and thanksgiving be to you, O almighty God and Father! For your protection and blessing, and for all the good which I have enjoyed during this past day! I would gladly enter the inner sanctum of my heart to worship you in spirit and truth. But it is still so full of impurity, for today I have been burdened with many scattered thoughts. Also, in my actions and life, I have not responded in the best way, for I am full of defects and mistakes; I am poor and miserable.

Although I am only dust and ashes, I still have dared to call upon your holy name. I pray and woefully implore you, O my God! Forgive me all my transgressions and mistakes with which I have offended you. Cleanse [256] my heart of all fleshly and worldly desires! Fill me with your Holy Spirit! Illuminate me with your light of grace! Thus may I come to know how my hidden mistakes look in the light.

Truly soften my heart, making it the bearer of remorse and sorrow. Through your grace bring about true regret and repentance in my soul. Give me the true, living, and saving faith. Kindle the fire of your divine love in my soul, and let it glow and burn until my selfishness is completely consumed.

I also pray for all people, for all the poor and unknown sinners, for all my enemies and opponents, for all the sick, for all the widows and the forsaken. You know the needs of each one, and may you aid each one who needs your help.

Now I lay my body down into the arms of your grace and mercy and commit myself, body and soul, into your hands. Protect me with your holy angels. Bless and shield me from all evil, whether I am asleep or awake. Teach me to reflect upon my nothingness, my dying, and my death. Finally receive my immortal soul into eternal joy and rest! This I pray, O almighty God and Father, in the name of Jesus Christ. Amen.

SUMMARY OF CONFESSION OF FAITH FROM A MENNONITE PERSPECTIVE

(North American, 1995)

❶ **We believe that God exists and is pleased with all who draw near by faith.** We worship the one holy and loving God who is Father, Son, and Holy Spirit eternally. God has created all things visible and invisible, has brought salvation and new life to humanity through Jesus Christ, and continues to sustain the church and all things until the end of the age.

❷ **We believe in Jesus Christ, the Word of God become flesh.** He is the Savior of the world, who has delivered us from the dominion of sin and reconciled us to God by his death on a cross. He was declared to be Son of God by his resurrection from the dead. He is the head of the church, the exalted Lord, the Lamb who was slain, coming again to reign with God in glory.

❸ **We believe in the Holy Spirit, the eternal Spirit of God,** who dwelled in Jesus Christ, who empowers the church, who is the source of our life in Christ, and who is poured out on those who believe as the guarantee of redemption.

❹ **We believe that all Scripture is inspired by God through the Holy Spirit for instruction in salvation and training in righteousness.** We accept the Scriptures as the Word of God and as the fully reliable and trustworthy standard for Christian faith and life. Led by the Holy Spirit in the church, we interpret Scripture in harmony with Jesus Christ.

5 We believe that God has created the heavens and the earth and all that is in them, and that God preserves and renews what has been made. All creation has its source outside itself and belongs to the Creator. The world has been created good because God is good and provides all that is needed for life.

6 We believe that God has created human beings in the divine image. God formed them from the dust of the earth and gave them a special dignity among all the works of creation. Human beings have been made for relationship with God, to live in peace with each other, and to take care of the rest of creation.

7 We confess that, beginning with Adam and Eve, humanity has disobeyed God, given way to the tempter, and chosen to sin. All have fallen short of the Creator's intent, marred the image of God in which they were created, disrupted order in the world, and limited their love for others. Because of sin, humanity has been given over to the enslaving powers of evil and death.

8 We believe that, through Jesus Christ, God offers salvation from sin and a new way of life. We receive God's salvation when we repent and accept Jesus Christ as Savior and Lord. In Christ, we are reconciled with God and brought into the reconciling community. We place our faith in God that, by the same power that raised Christ from the dead, we may be saved from sin to follow Christ and to know the fullness of salvation.

9 We believe that the church is the assembly of those who have accepted God's offer of salvation through faith in Jesus Christ. It is the new community of disciples sent into the world to proclaim the reign of God and to provide a foretaste of the church's glorious hope. It is the new society established and sustained by the Holy Spirit.

⑩ We believe that the mission of the church is to proclaim and to be a sign of the kingdom of God. Christ has commissioned the church to make disciples of all nations, baptizing them, and teaching them to observe all things he has commanded.

⑪ We believe that the baptism of believers with water is a sign of their cleansing from sin. Baptism is also a pledge before the church of their covenant with God to walk in the way of Jesus Christ through the power of the Holy Spirit. Believers are baptized into Christ and his body by the Spirit, water, and blood.

⑫ We believe that the Lord's Supper is a sign by which the church thankfully remembers the new covenant which Jesus established by his death. In this communion meal, the church renews its covenant with God and with each other and participates in the life and death of Jesus Christ, until he comes.

⑬ We believe that in washing the feet of his disciples, Jesus calls us to serve one another in love as he did. Thus we acknowledge our frequent need of cleansing, renew our willingness to let go of pride and worldly power, and offer our lives in humble service and sacrificial love.

⑭ We practice discipline in the church as a sign of God's offer of transforming grace. Discipline is intended to liberate erring brothers and sisters from sin and to restore them to a right relationship with God and to fellowship in the church. The practice of discipline gives integrity to the church's witness in the world.

⑮ We believe that ministry is a continuation of the work of Christ, who gives gifts through the Holy Spirit to all believers and empowers them for service in the church and in the world. We also believe that God calls particular persons in the church to specific leadership ministries and offices. All who minister are accountable to God and to the community of faith.

16 We believe that the church of Jesus Christ is one body with many members, ordered in such a way that, through the one Spirit, believers may be built together spiritually into a dwelling place for God.

17 We believe that Jesus Christ calls us to discipleship, to take up our cross and follow him. Through the gift of God's saving grace, we are empowered to be disciples of Jesus, filled with his Spirit, following his teachings and his path through suffering to new life. As we are faithful to his way, we become conformed to Christ and separated from the evil in the world.

18 We believe that to be a disciple of Jesus is to know life in the Spirit. As the life, death, and resurrection of Jesus Christ takes shape in us, we grow in the image of Christ and in our relationship with God. The Holy Spirit is active in individual and in communal worship, leading us deeper into the experience of God.

19 We believe that God intends human life to begin in families and to be blessed through families. Even more, God desires all people to become part of the church, God's family. As single and married members of the church family give and receive nurture and healing, families can grow toward the wholeness that God intends. We are called to chastity and to loving faithfulness in marriage.

20 We commit ourselves to tell the truth, to give a simple yes or no, and to avoid the swearing of oaths.

㉑ We believe that everything belongs to God, who calls the church to live in faithful stewardship of all that God has entrusted to us, and to participate now in the rest and justice which God has promised.

㉒ We believe that peace is the will of God. God created the world in peace, and God's peace is most fully revealed in Jesus Christ, who is our peace and the peace of the whole world. Led by the Holy Spirit, we follow Christ in the way of peace, doing justice, bringing reconciliation, and practicing nonresistance, even in the face of violence and warfare.

㉓ We believe that the church is God's holy nation, called to give full allegiance to Christ its head and to witness to every nation, government, and society about God's saving love.

㉔ We place our hope in the reign of God and its fulfillment in the day when Christ will come again in glory to judge the living and the dead. He will gather his church, which is already living under the reign of God. We await God's final victory, the end of this present age of struggle, the resurrection of the dead, and a new heaven and a new earth. There the people of God will reign with Christ in justice, righteousness, and peace forever and ever.

Adopted by the delegates of Mennonite Church General Assembly, and of the General Conference Mennonite Church Triennial Session, July 28, 1995, Wichita, Kansas. Mennonite Church USA, formed by the merger of these two groups, has adopted this confession as its statement of faith.

MENNONITE WORLD CONFERENCE CORE CONVICTIONS

(Global, 2006)

By the grace of God we seek to live and proclaim the good news of reconciliation in Jesus Christ. As part of one body of Christ at all times and places, we hold the following to be central to our belief and practice:

1. God is known to us as Father, Son and Holy Spirit, the Creator who seeks to restore fallen humanity by calling a people to be faithful in fellowship, worship, service and witness.

2. Jesus is the Son of God. Through his life and teaching, his cross and resurrection he showed how to be faithful disciples, redeemed the world, and offered eternal life.

3. As a church we are a community of those whom God's Spirit calls to turn from sin, acknowledge Jesus Christ as Lord, receive baptism upon confession of faith and follow Christ in life.

4. As a faith community, we accept the Bible as our authority for faith and life, interpreting it together under Holy Spirit guidance in the light of Jesus Christ to discern God's will for our obedience.

5. The Spirit of Jesus empowers us to trust God in all areas of life as we become peacemakers who renounce violence, love our enemies, seek justice, and share our possessions with those in need.

6 We gather regularly to worship, to celebrate the Lord's Supper, and to hear the Word of God in a spirit of mutual accountability.

7 As a worldwide family of faith and life we transcend boundaries of nationality, race, class, gender, and language and seek to live in the world as a global community without conforming to the powers of evil, witnessing to God's grace by serving others, caring for creation, and inviting all people to know Jesus as Savior and Lord.

In these convictions we draw inspiration from Anabaptist forbears of the sixteenth century, who modeled radical discipleship to Jesus Christ. Walking in his name and aware of our continuing need of the power of the Holy Spirit, we confidently await Christ's return and the final fulfillment of God's Kingdom.

Adopted by Mennonite World Conference,
Pasadena, California, 2006.

FOR FURTHER READING

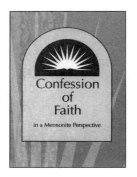

Confession of Faith in a Mennonite Perspective. 1995, 112 pages. This confession guides the faith and life of the Mennonite Church Canada and the Mennonite Church USA.

Confesión de Fe en una Perspectiva Menonita. 2000, 132 paginas. Este confesión guia la fe y la vida de la Iglesia Menonita Canada y la Iglesia Menonita USA.

Beliefs: Mennonite Faith and Practice by John D. Roth. 2004, 150 pages. This short, engaging book gives a brief account of what Mennonites believe. Roth provides solid framework for conversations about faithful discipleship.

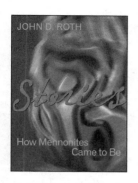

Stories: How Mennonites Came to Be by John D. Roth. 2006, 246 pages. Amid conflict and commitment, Mennonites trace their stories from the New Testament church on the day of Pentecost to the global community of the 21st century.

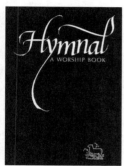

Hymnal: A Worship Book. 1992, 904 pages. 658 hymns and 202 worship resources representing a variety of styles and settings, with two supplements: **Sing the Journey** (2005) and **Sing the Story** (2007).

Take Our Moments and Our Days: An Anabaptist Prayer Book edited by Arthur Paul Boers, Barbara Nelson Gingerich, Eleanor Kreider, John D. Rempel, Mary H. Schertz. 2007, 384 pages. A four-week cycle of morning and evening prayer services prepared for the period in the church year between Pentecost and Advent.

Publications available from Herald Press. To order or request information, please call 1-800-245-7894, or visit www.heraldpress.com.

NOTES AND STUFF

NOTES AND STUFF

"This is a practical and down-to-earth guide for anyone new to a Mennonite congregation. It covers basic beliefs, practices and the essential history of the Mennonites. But this is just the beginning. Where else can you find advice on how to stay alert in church, the meaning of baptism, communion and foot washing, sharing your faith and the text of the Schleitheim Confession—all between two covers?"

    —Craig Carter, Tyndale University, Ontario

"This concise anthology of the Mennonite history, beliefs, and practices is a rich mine of . . . ah, forget it—it's a hoot! Rookies will get questions answered and veterans will nod in appreciation as the mystery of 'What's up with us!?!' gets unpackaged in this clever and easy-to-read book. Enjoy!"

    —Steve "Reece" Friesen, Eben-Ezer Mennonite Church, British Columbia

"A handbook with a sense of humor, as well as filled with wisdom."

    —Stanley Hauerwas, Duke University

"A great gift to the church."

    —Wayne Hochstetler, Illinois Mennonite Conference

"I like the humor . . . I appreciate an amazingly accurate portrayal of some of the awkward truths of the Mennonite Church."

    —Elizabeth Miller, State College Mennonite, Pennsylvania